BASIC ITALIAN

Instructions, Cultural Notes and Conversations

By

Imma Trisorio Keith

© 1999, 2003 by Imma Trisorio Keith. All rights reserved.

No part of this book may be reproduced, stored in a retrieval system, or transmitted by any means, electronic, mechanical, photocopying, recording, or otherwise, without written permission from the author.

ISBN: 1-4107-3363-7 (e-book)
ISBN: 1-4107-3362-9 (Paperback)

This book is printed on acid free paper.

INTRODUCTION

Una breve spiegazione dei diversi dialetti:

There are many different dialects used in Italy, but there is one standard national language. What is so interesting about Italian dialects is the fact that a person from one region does not understand the dialect of another region. If a Neapolitan goes to Sicily and hears only dialect spoken, he or she has no more chance to understand it, than a person from a different country.

Most people speak the national language plus the dialect of their native area. The dialect is more likely used by older generations, while the young generations tend to use the Italian language. The language used in the media, radio, newspapers and television, is the standard national language.

Each region of Italy has its own accent as well, which is very different from dialect.
A dialect from one region can be and often is so different from the dialect of another region, that it is like speaking French versus Spanish. The accent is only indicative of the native region of the speaker, eventhough it sometimes includes words used in one region and not in another, keeping the meaning clear. Those slight differences, referred to as accents, exist almost everywhere. For example in the South of the United States it is common to hear 'y'all' versus 'you guys' in the West U.S.

The diversity of the dialects is generally divided into four areas:

1. The North, excluding the Veneto province, including Piemonte, Liguria, Lombardia etc.
2. Tuscan, which is subdivided into three groups: central Tuscany, Florence; Pisa, Livorno, Lucca on the west, and Siena, Arezzo on the south.
3. Central, including Lazio, Umbria e Marche provinces.
4. South, including Abruzzi, Campania, Lucania, e Puglia, Calabria e Sicilia provinces.

In Sardenia there is yet another dialect spoken. It is not unusual to find, in the small town of the south, people who speak only the dialect. In the Basilicata, a region in the south of Italy, there are people who speak the Albanian language, mostly because originally their ancestors came from Albania, and the language or now dialect has been passed from generation to generation.

Cultural differences also exist in the various regions of Italy. Even the cooking is very different from region to region. The national culture is enriched by the diversity of the many local cultures.

Italian, rather than the dialect, is being used more and more throughout Italy, as a language not only written but spoken as well. As a spoken language it has regional varieties or accents, expressed mostly in the pronunciation. It is the language used in the schools and in the communication media.

Less than a decade ago not many American tourists even tried to learn the language. In recent years there has been an explosion of tourism in Europe, especially Italy, such that in Florence there is discussion about a reservation system to visit the most famous sites as a way to control the number of tourists in each place. Also in recent years there have been more American tourists or military personnel stationed there, speaking the language, a fact that is very much appreciated by the Italians. In the large cities it is not uncommon to find many merchants speaking English, but being able to converse with an Italian in Italian is a pleasant experience.

How to use this book:

This book includes grammar, text written in Italian and English for practice purposes, cultural notes of general interest, a review of the first fourteen chapters. Verbs, a complete conjugation of the verb 'parlare', few words on traditions, idioms, and some examples of conversation when buying a train ticket or ordering a meal in an Italian restaurant. It also has a chapter of short stories, written both in Italian and English, and lastly a key to the exercises.

The objective of this book is to teach a student the basic grammar of the Italian language, by showing the structure of a sentence and the formation of the various tenses in the conjugation of the regular verbs. Once the student acquires the knowledge of how to form a sentence and some basic verb conjugation, he or she can expand at his or her pace.

The responsibility of the student is to study the material and practice, practice, practice.
It is good a good idea to do the exercises, listed at the end of most chapters, and even doing them over to understand the structure. It is recommended to learn the sounds of the vowels very well and other sounds, which are so different and often opposite in the English language.

For those who commute or have the additional time, tapes in Italian can be of help. There are a number of tapes available, either through local libraries or bookstores. The pronunciation is acquired by practice, so more time spent on this topic, the better the results.

TABLE OF CONTENTS

		Page
Introduction	A brief explanation of existing dialects	iii
Chapter 1	Alphabet & pronunciation - Practice.	1
Chapter 2	Gender of nouns, definite & indefinite articles – Practice & Exercises	7
Chapter 3	Verbs & pronouns – Practice – Vocabulary Exercises	13
Chapter 4	Auxiliary verbs 'Essere & Avere' & some irregular verbs such as 'Fare, Andare, Dovere' – Practice – Vocabulary - Exercises	21
Chapter 5	Adjectives & Agreement with nouns, possessive adjectives. Exercises	33
Chapter 6	Cultural notes for practical purpose, a basic conversation	43
Chapter 7	The verb 'Stare' & the use of 'LEI' as a polite way of addressing a person. Exercises	49
Chapter 8	A visit to Siena	57
Chapter 9	Prepositions, more on verbs, past participle. Exercises	69
Chapter 10	Comparisons of adjectives. Exercises	79
Chapter 11	The numbers, time of day, exchange. Exercises	87
Chapter 12	Foods - Wines	95
Chapter 13	Tenses of verbs – future tense. Exercise	109
Chapter 14	Verbs – Future tense of helping verbs. Exercise	117
Chapter 15	Review	125
Chapter 16	The legend of S. Gennaro, Patron of Naples and the 'Explosion of the Cart' on Easter Sunday in Florence	135
Chapter 17	Reflexive verbs	143

Chapter 18	Additional reflexive verbs	151
Chapter 19	Simple tenses of verbs, 'conditional and gerund'	161
Chapter 20	Object pronouns	169
Chapter 21	Additional tenses of verbs and their application	177
Chapter 22	Adverbs and their function, and conjunctions	185
Chapter 23	Compound tenses (various)	197
Chapter 24	Compound tenses for reflexive verbs	207
Chapter 25	Complete conjugation in all tenses of the verb 'Parlare'	213
Chapter 26	A few words about tradition and a conversation	221
Chapter 27	Agreement of gender when using past participle	229
Chapter 28	Idioms and examples of application	235
Chapter 29	How to order a meal in an Italian restaurant and how to buy a train ticket.	249
Chapter 30	Short stories written in Italian and translated in English	257
Key to Exercises		273

BASIC ITALIAN
Instructions, Cultural Notes and Conversations

CAPITOLO UNO (1)

L'alfabeto e la pronuncia.

ch = K

Vowels are important and those are: a, e, i, o, u the pronunciation is:
- a as in father, arm
- e as in get, net
- i as in feed, seat e
- o as in bowl, toe
- u as in tube, dude

The Italian alphabet has 21 letters:

Letter:	Name:	Pronunciation:	Letter:	Name:	Pronunciation:	Letter:	Name:	Pronunciation:
a	a	/ah/	h	acca	/akkah/	q	cu	/koo/
b	bi	/bee/	i	i	/ee/	r	erre	/ehrray/
c	ci	/chee/	l	elle	/ehllay/	s	esse	/ehssay/
d	di	/dee/	m	emme	/ehmmay/	t	ti	/tee/
e	e	/eh/	n	enne	/ehnnay/	u	u	/oo/
f	effe	/ehffay/	o	o	/oh/	v	vu	/voo/
g	gi	/jee/	p	pi	/pee/	z	zeta	/dzehtah/

There are five more letters, which are found in words of latin or foreign origin, and those are: j (i lunga), k (cappa), w (v doppia), x (ics), y (ipsilon).

Pronunciation:

The letter '**h**' is silent, for example: words such as hanno (they have) and anno (year) sound alike, however have different meanings. The context of the sentence will indicate the right one.

The letters '**c and g**', when used in front of **e and i**, have a soft sound, such as:

NOTES

Che Si Mangia? What's to eat

Che Si Mancia? - what's the tip

Che Pensi? - what do you think

Arrivederci - Good-by is proper Italian   Ciao - hello or goodby

Il Pranzo è Buono - Good dinner

Che Buon Pranzo - what a good dinner

Carne - Meat?

Cena - supper

Cinque - five

il Conto - bill

Cura - cure

BASIC ITALIAN
Instructions, Cultural Notes and Conversations

	Pronunciation:	Meaning:			
c + e = cena	/chehna/ -	(supper)	c + i = cima	/chima/ -	(top)
c + e = cereale	/chehrehale/ -	(cereal)	c + i = cinema	/chinema/ -	(cinema)
c + e = cera	/chehra/ -	(wax)	c + i = cinque	/cheenque/ -	(five)
g + e = gelato	/jehlato/	(ice cream)	g + i = giro	/jeero/	(turn)
g + e = generale	/jehenehraleh/	(general)	g + i = gita	/jeeta/	(excursion)
g + e = gentile	/jehnteele/	(kind)	g + i = ginnasio	/jeennaseeo/	(gymnasium)

'The letters **'c and g'** when used in front of **a, o, u,** have a hard sound, such as:

c + a = casa	/kasa/	(house)	c + o = cosa	/kosa/	(thing)
c + a = cara	/kara/	(dear)	c + o = costo	/kosto/	(cost)
c + a = castello	/kastehllo/	(castle)	c + o = conto	/konto/	(bill)
c + u = cura	/koora/	(cure)	c + u = culla	/koolla/	(cradle)
c + u = curioso	/kooreeoso/	(curious)			
g + a = galleria	/gallehreea/	(gallery)	g + o = gola	/ghola/	(throat)
g + a = gara	/ghara/	(competition)	g + o = goccia	ghoccheea/	(drop)
g + a = garofano	/garofano/	(carnation)	g + o = governo	/ghoverno/	(government)
g + u = guanto	/gooanto/	(glove)	g + u = guscio	/goosheeo/	(shell)
g + u = gusto	/goosto/	(taste)			

Above pronunciation rules are the same even if above combinations appear in the middle or at the end of the words. For example: sempli**ce** (simple), fidu**cia** (trust), vo**ca**le (vowel), botte**ga** (shop).

Words ending in **ca or ga** in the singular, become **che or ghe** in the plural, in order to maintain the same sound (k), for example: amica becomes amiche (friends, fem.) - lega becomes leghe (leagues).

NOTES

OGGI É UNA BELLA GIORNATE — today is a beautiful day
(Today is a / beautiful day)

CHE BELLA GIORNATA — what a beautiful day

The letters **ch** are used only followed by **e or i** and it has a hard sound like english k, for example: chi, /kee/, (who), che, /keh/, (what), chiodo, /keeodo/, (nail), chiesa, /keeehsa/, (church).

The letters **gh** are used only followed by **e or i** and it has a hard sound like English g as in good, for example: ghiaccio /gheeaccheeo/ (ice), lunghezza /loonghehzza/, (length).

The letters **gl** are pronounced close to double **ll** in English, for example: famiglia /fameelleea/ (family).

Words with double letters need to be pronounced a little stronger than those with one letter, otherwise they may have a different meaning, for example: capello /kapehllo/ (hair), cappello /kappehllo/ (hat).

Practice the pronunciation of the following words:

Ciao	(hello or bye)	cinema	(cinema)
cucina	(kitchen)	cura	(cure)
gelato	(ice cream)	giro	(turn)
galleria	(gallery)	guanto	(glove)
chi	(who)	che	(what)
ghiaccio	(ice)	lunghezza	(length)
larghezza	(width)	gente	(people)
giardino	(garden)	rosa	(rose or pink)
rossa	(red)	gioco	(game)
giusto	(right)	cioccolato	(chocolate)
gusto	(taste)	gamba	(leg)
conto	(bill)	casa	(house)
cosa	(thing)	che cosa	(what thing)
che	(what)	come	(how, what)
giorno	(day)	gentile	(kind)
ghiotto	(glutton)	giusto	(right)

NOTES

Bambino - 1 baby
Bambini - 2 or more boys
Bambina - 1 girl
Bambine - 2 or more girls

BASIC ITALIAN
Instructions, Cultural Notes and Conversations

CAPITOLO DUE (2)

I sostantivi e gli articoli.

In Italian nouns have gender, and it is imperative to be able to determine the gender of a noun in order to construct a correct sentence, because adjectives and articles will have to agree with the gender of the noun, as we will see later on in this book.

Words ending with '**o**' are masculine, for example: gelato, Mario, giardino.

Words ending with '**a**' are feminine, for example: gamba, Maria, galleria.

Words ending with '**e**' can be either, the context of the sentence will show the gender or sometimes the word itself will indicate the gender, for example: padre (father), madre (mother), nipote (nephew or niece).

Another way to determine the gender of words ending in '**e**' is to look up that word in the Italian-English dictionary as it will show the gender in parenthesis next to the word.

Examples: giardino - conto - gelato - ghiaccio - guanto - vino: all masculine nouns

gamba - galleria - casa - cassa - culla - bambina: all feminine nouns

padre (m) - madre (f) - fiore (m) – nipote   (can be either masc. or fem.)

All of the above nouns are in the singular, there is also a plural for each of the categories, as follows:

Masculine nouns, which end in '**o**' in the singular, end in '**i**' in the plural.

Feminine nouns, which end in '**a**' in the singular, end in '**e**' in the plural.

All words ending in '**e**' in the singular, **always** end in '**i**' in the plural, regardless of gender.

Examples: giardini - conti - gelati - guanti - vini - bambini: all masc. plural nouns
(gardens) (bills) (ice cream) (gloves) (wines) (children)

gambe - gallerie - case - casse - culle - bambine: all fem. plural nouns
(legs) (galleries) (houses) (registers) (cribs) (children)

padri - madri - fiori - nipoti - conversazioni - stazioni: plural nouns of either gender.
(fathers, masc.) (mothers, fem.) (flowers, masc.) (nephews or nieces) (conversations, fem.) (stations, fem.)

7

NOTES

IL GIORNO - The day   UN - a day
I GIORNI - The days

LA CASA - The house   UNA CASA - a house
LE CASE - The houses

IL VINO - wine
I VINI - the wines

TI VOGLIO BENE - I love you - friend, child

TI AMO - husband, wife

           Come sta / how are you → BENE, GRAZIE
VOLERE   COME STAI? /   Fine, thank you
↓
to want

COME - TI CHIAMI?

Come - Si Chiama

COME - SI DICE -
(what) how do you say

The definite Article:

When an article is used with a noun, it has to agree with the noun in gender and whether it is singular or plural:

Masculine singular article: **il - lo - l'** (English the)

Masculine plural article: **i - gli** "

Feminine singular article: **la - l'** "

Feminine plural article: **le -** "

il is used in front of singular masculine nouns, ex: il giardino.

lo is used in front of singular masculine nouns beginning with s + consonant, or z, or ps, or pn, or gn. ex: lo studente, lo zio (uncle.)

l' is used in front of singular masculine nouns beginning with a vowel, ex: l'amico (friend)

i is used in front of plural masculine nouns, ex: i giardini.

gli is used in front of plural masculine nouns beginning with a vowel, ex: gli Italiani.

la is used in front of singular feminine nouns, ex: la gamba.

l' is used in front of singular feminine nouns beginning with a vowel, ex: l'amica (friend)

le is used in front of plural feminine nouns, ex: le case.

The indefinite Article:

Masculine singular article: **un, uno** (a, an)

Feminine singular article: **una, un'** "

un is used in front of singular masculine nouns, ex: un guanto (a glove)

uno is used in front of singular masculine nouns beginning with s +consonant, or z, or ps, or pn, or gn, ex: uno studente, uno zio.

una is used in front of singular feminine nouns, ex: una cosa (a thing)

NOTES

BASIC ITALIAN
Instructions, Cultural Notes and Conversations

un' is used in front of singular feminine nouns beginning with a vowel, ex: un'idea.

i disabili (dee-SAH-bee-lee)
the disabled

LIVING LANGUAGE

articles and nouns:

ambini, le bambine, il ghiaccio, la casa, la miche, la gara, le gare, il fiore, i fiori, il li spumoni, un gioco, un giorno, l'uovo, lo

ouns: *Sing + pl.*   *Homework*

lcolatori   cucina - cucine

C'è la toilette per i disabili?
Is there a bathroom for the handicapped?

(culator)   21. Cucina (kitchen)
ctive)   22. Pentola (pan)
e)   23. Cucchiaio (spoon)
g)   24. Coltello (knife)
ificate)   25. Piatto (plate)
            26. Tazza (cup)
helf)   27. Bicchiere (glass) *no*
or niece)   28. Acqua (water)
            29. Bottiglia (bottle)
            30. Cappuccino (coffee & milk)

Tuesday/martedì **25** September/settembre

Exercise 2.

Example: la finestra, la sedia. i calcolatori, gli aggettivi una cucina, una pentola

Place the correct definite article to the first ten nouns above, keeping them in the singular.
Place the correct definite article to the second ten nouns after converting them to plural.
Place the correct indefinite article to the third ten nouns.

NOTES

BASIC ITALIAN
Instructions, Cultural Notes and Conversations

CAPITOLO TRE (3)

I verbi e la coniugazione.

The verbs in the Italian language are very different from those in English. The conjugation and the various tenses require some effort to learn and memorize. Pay particular attention to the ending of each word as it will determine the person intended, as the student will see.

Also because the ending of each word in the conjugation indicates the person or the subject, the usage of pronouns is usually omitted, but it is correct to use them, just not necessary in many cases. However, if it helps to learn and memorize the conjugation, the student is encouraged to do so.

Most verbs end in '**are**' - '**ere**' - '**ire**' ex: ascol**tare** (to listen) - prend**ere** (to take) - sent**ire** (to hear or feel). The stem of the verb is, usually, present in all the tenses.

To determine the stem of any verb, simply remove the ending, ex: ascoltare - the stem is '**ascolt**' - prendere - the stem is '**prend**' - sentire - the stem is '**sent**'. Since in the dictionaries the verbs are listed in the infinitive tense, being able to determine the stem of the verb, allows the student to conjugate any verb, by changing the endings. Usually the stem of the verb is present throughout the conjugation, just the ending changes.

There are regular and irregular verbs, with the majority being regular. The first presentation in this chapter will deal with the regular verbs and later on the others. It will be clear to determine the difference.

Pronouns are used in lieu of names. There are subject and object pronouns and there are several. You will see the basic ones at first, keeping in mind that the objective of the introduction of the pronouns at this time, is to facilitate the learning of the conjugation of Italian verbs.

Practice reading the following paragraph, focusing on the usage of the verbs:

Mario **ascolta** la radio quando la madre ritorna a casa. Mario domanda alla
madre: 'Mamma, **prendi** un caffe'?' 'Si, grazie, Mario' risponde la madre.
Mario prepara un bel caffe' per la madre, che si **sente** molto stanca.

Mario listens to the radio when the mother returns home. Mario asks the mother
'Mom, will you have a cup of coffee?' 'Yes, thank you, Mario' answers the
mother. Mario prepares a nice cup of coffee for the mother, who feels very tired.

NOTES

BASIC ITALIAN
Instructions, Cultural Notes and Conversations

SAMPLES OF VERBS ENDING IN ARE, ERE, IRE AND PRONOUNS:

Ascoltare = To Listen

<u>Present Tense</u>

Pronouns: Verb:

io	ascolto	(I listen)	noi	ascoltiamo	(we listen)
tu	ascolti	(you listen)	voi	ascoltate	(you, pl, listen)
lui, lei	ascolta	(he, she listens)	loro	ascoltano	(they listen)

Prendere = To Take

<u>Present Tense</u>

io	prendo	(I take)	noi	prendiamo	(we take)
tu	prendi	(you take)	voi	prendete	(you, pl, take)
lui, lei	prende	(he, she takes)	loro	prendono	(they take)

Sentire = To Hear or to Feel

<u>Present Tense</u>

io	sento	(I hear)	noi	sentiamo	(we hear)
tu	senti	(you hear)	voi	sentite	(you, pl, hear)
lui, lei	sente	(he, she hears)	loro	sentono	(they hear)

Note: When the verb 'sentire' is used to mean 'to feel', it is used in the reflexive form, which will be covered lateron.

Pronouns: the subject pronoun for the second person **'tu'** (you) is used when referring to one person.
The subject pronoun for the second person **'voi'** (you) is used when referring to two or more persons.

NOTES

La Macchina - "Car"

BASIC ITALIAN
Instructions, Cultural Notes and Conversations

There are three types of subject pronouns for the third person, which are: **egli, ella / lui, lei/ esso, essa;** each type has its function. Egli, Ella are used in more formal speaking or writing; lui, lei are used in informal speaking or writing, and esso, essa can be used for either.

The following subject pronouns are used when referring to people egli, ella/ lui, lei (used in the above conjugation) and esso, essa all meaning **he** or **she**.
The following pronouns are used when referring to things or animals / esso, essa meaning **it**.
Esso, essi, essa, esse is the only pronoun that can be used for either people or things.

Practice the pronunciation of the following sentences:

Maria ascolta la radio
(Maria listens to the radio)

Io ascolto il maestro
(I listen to the teacher)

Bambino, ascolti
(Little boy, listen)

Mario prende un caffe'
(Mario has a coffee)

Io prendo una coca cola
(I have a coke)

Tu prendi una pentola
(You get a cooking pot)

Io sento un rumore
(I hear a noise)

Lei sente la radio
(She hears the radio)

Noi sentiamo la macchina
(We hear the car)

Essi sentono la musica
(They hear the music)

Noi ascoltiamo la musica
(We listen to the music)

Voi ascoltate la televisione
(You listen to TV)

Essi ascoltano la guida
(They listen to the guide)

Noi prendiamo il latte
(We have milk)

Voi prendete un cappuccino
(You have a cappuccino)

I bambini prendono il latte
The children have milk)

Tu senti un uccello
(You hear a bird)

Lui sente un rumore
(He hears a noise)

Voi sentite la TV
(You hear the TV)

Esse sentono il telefono
(They hear the phone)

NOTES

Neonato - infant

Ragazzi - Boys

BASIC ITALIAN
Instructions, Cultural Notes and Conversations

Vocabulary:

Ragazze - Girls

Sedile	-	Seat	Cugino	-	Cousin	Ghiaccio	- Ice
Macchina	-	Car	Madre	-	Mother	Gelato	- Ice Cream
Treno	-	Train	Padre	-	Father	Focaccia	- Italian bread
Tassi'	-	Taxi	Fratello	-	Brother	Pasta	- Pasta
Carrozza	-	Train car	Sorella	-	Sister	Zucchero	- Sugar

Exercise 3:

Match the sentences in column one with those in column two.

1. Lei sente i bambini.
2. Cathy ascolta la radio.
3. I bambini ascoltano la madre.
4. Io prendo un biscotto.
5. Loro prendono il ghiaccio.
6. Io sento il telefono.

a. They take ice. 5
b. The children listen to the mother. 3
c. I have a cookie. 4
d. I hear the phone. 6
e. She hears the children. 1
f. Caterina listens to the radio. 2

NOTES

DOVE SEI? – Where are you

STANCA – tired

FELICE – happy

TRISTE – SAD

IO OGGI sono A CASA = At Home

SEI BRAVO = Well done

Io sono stanca – I am tired
Io non sono stanca – Not tired

OGGI – TODAY

NOI SIAMO TUTTI IN CLASSE   We are all in class

No – No
Si – yes

　　　　　　　　　Sorelle – due Sisters
UNA – A　　UNA Sorella – A sister
UN – A　　UN Fratello – A brother
UNO – 1　　Due Fratelli – 2 brothers
DUE – 2
TRE – 3
e = and
è = is
Quattro – 4

BASIC ITALIAN
Instructions, Cultural Notes and Conversations

CAPITOLO QUATTRO (4)

I verbi ausiliari e la coniugazione.

The auxiliary verbs 'essere' (to be) and 'avere' (to have) are an essential part of the conjugation of verbs in general. These verbs can be used by themselves or in conjunction with other verbs as auxiliary or, more commonly, called helping verbs.

Essere = To Be					
		Present Tense			
io	sono	(I am)	noi	siamo	(we are)
tu	sei	(you are)	voi	siete	(you, pl, are)
lui, lei	e'	(he, she is)	loro	sono	(they are)

Avere = To Have					
		Present Tense			
io	ho	(I have)	noi	abbiamo	(we have)
tu	hai	(you have)	voi	avete	(you, pl, have)
lui, lei	ha	(he, she has)	loro	hanno	(they have)

h is silent - needs to be written not said

Practice reading the paragraph in Italian and determine the forms of the auxiliary verbs used.

Luigi ha una bella famiglia e nella sua famiglia ci sono sette persone; il padre, la madre, due sorelle, e tre fratelli. Luigi e' il piu' piccolo. Una sorella di Luigi e' sposata ed ha due bambini, tutti e due maschi. La sorella sposata di Luigi abita lontano e viene a casa dei genitori per le feste. Luigi dice: siamo tanto felici quando siamo tutti insieme. La madre di Luigi dice: sono molto contenta, quando ho tutta la famiglia insieme a casa mia.

Non c'è ~~male~~ - not to bad
Non c'è male - not to bad

NOTES

CHE FAI? what you doing?

i ~~com~~ COMPITI = Homework

LA PAGINA DEL LIBRO
IL FIGLIO DELLA DONNA - the son of the ~~mother~~ woman

DELLA = of the

di - of

Luigi has a nice family and in his family there are seven persons; the father, the mother, two sisters, and three brothers. Luigi is the youngest. One of Luigi's sisters is married and has two boys. Luigi's married sister lives far and comes to her parents' house for holidays. Luigi says: we are so happy when we are all together. Luigi's mother says: I am very content when I have all my family at my house.

Verbs can be transitive and intransitive, some verbs can be either, depending on its use and function in a particular sentence. **Transitive** verbs are those which can take an object such as: Mangio una mela (I eat an apple). **Intransitive** verbs are those which **do not** take an object such as: camminare (to walk).

Usually, when the verbs **'essere' and 'avere'** are used as **helping verbs,** the general rule of thumb is: the **transitive** verbs are conjugated with the verb **'avere'** (to have) and the **intransitive** verbs are conjugated with the verb **'essere'** (to be). Occasionally some verbs can be either transitive or intransitive depending on the context of the sentence.

Irregular verbs have a conjugation of their own and do not follow the same rules as the regular verbs. Therefore the only way to learn them is to memorize them, because each irregular verb conjugation is pretty much unique to that particular verb. Following is the conjugation of three common irregular verbs:

Fare = To Make or To Do

Present Tense

io	faccio	(I make)	noi	facciamo	(we make)
tu	fai	(you make)	voi	fate	(you, pl. make)
lui, lei	fa	(he, she makes)	loro	fanno	(they make)

NOTES

Danno - damage
Temporale - storm
Vento - wind
Alberi - trees

ORE = hours
ORA - hour or now

AVUTO - had

Avete ~~avet~~ avuto danni - you (all) had damages

AVETE Perso L'ELETRICITA - Have you lost electricity

PER QUANTE ORE? How many hours

AVETE PERSO Alberi - have you lost trees

IO NON Ho PERSO AlBERI - have not lost trees

Pioggia = Rain
Piovere = to Rain

C'È IL SOLE = there is sunshine

TEMPO - WEATHER

PAZZO = CRAZY   AL FRESCO - Shade

BASTA - Enough
NEVE - snow

L'AGGETTIVO'

PAPA = POPE
PAPÀ = DAD

FAME = HUNGER
SETE = ~~Feter~~ Thirst

Andare = To Go

Present Tense

io	vado	(I go)
tu	vai	(you go)
lui, lei	va	(he, she goes)
noi	andiamo	(we go) *let's go*
voi	andate	(you, pl, go)
loro	vanno	(they go)

Dovere = To Owe or To Have to or To Be obliged to or must

Present Tense

io	devo	(I owe)
tu	devi	(you owe)
lui, lei	deve	(he, she owes)
noi	dobbiamo	(we owe)
voi	dovete	(you, pl, owe)
loro	devono	(they owe)

NOTES

BASIC ITALIAN
Instructions, Cultural Notes and Conversations

Practice reading the following sentences, focusing on the verbs:

Io sono italiana.	(I am Italian)	Io ho una mela.	(I have an apple)
Tu sei americano.	(You are American)	Tu hai la casa.	(You have a house)
Esso e' un cane maschio.	(It is a male dog)	Lui ha la gatta.	(He has the cat, fem.)
Essa e' una gatta.	(It is a female cat)	Lei ha la madre.	(She has the mother)
Noi siamo a casa.	(we are at home)	Noi abbiamo un fratello	(We have a brother)
Voi siete piccoli.	(You, pl, are small)	Voi avete fame.	(You, pl., are hungry)
Loro sono in cucina.	(They are in the kitchen)	Loro hanno sete.	(They are thirsty)

Io faccio bene.	(I do well)	Io vado a casa.	(I go home)
Tu fai male.	(You do bad)	Tu vai alla spiaggia.	(You go to the beach)
Lui fa il pane.	(He makes the bread)	Lei va alla spiaggia.	(She goes to the beach)
Noi facciamo il caffe.	(We make the coffee)	Noi andiamo al cinema.	(we go to the movies)
Voi fate la torta.	(You, pl., make the cake)	Voi andate via.	(You, pl., go away)
Loro fanno la pasta.	(They make the pasta)	Loro vanno al teatro.	(They go to the theater)

NOTES

Io	devo molti soldi.	(I owe a lot of money)
Tu	devi andare.	(You must go)
Lui	deve lavorare.	(He must work)
Lei	deve un favore.	(She owes a favor)
Noi	dobbiamo andare.	(We must go)
Voi	dovete essere bravi.	(You, pl., must be good)
Loro	devono fare i piatti	(They must do dishes)
Loro	devono avere soldi	(They must have money)

Vocabulary:

Teatro	-	Theater	Sale	-	Salt	Di -	Of or From
Fuori	-	Outside	Pepe	-	Pepper	Da -	From
Dentro	-	Inside	Torta	-	Cake	In -	In
Fra or Tra -		Among	Pane	-	bread	a -	At or To

Exercise 4:

Usare il verbo necessario nelle frasi seguenti (Use the necessary verb in the following sentences):

1. Maria _____ fame.
2. Mario _____ sete.
3. Giorgio _____ un ragazzo italiano.
4. Quante sorelle _____ Teresa?
5. I signori _____ un accento italiano.
6. Il cappuccino _____ freddo.
7. Il cane _____ bello.
8. Il cane _____ maschio.
9. Noi _____ un fratello.
10. Voi _____ un gatto.

NOTES

BASIC ITALIAN
Instructions, Cultural Notes and Conversations

Exercise 5:

Match the following sentences:

1. Noi abbiamo fame. _e_
2. Teresa ha una sorella. _d_
3. La madre di Mario e' a casa. _b_
4. Io ho un fratello. _c_
5. Loro sono al cinema. _a_

a. They are at the movies. _5_
b. Mario's mother is at home. _3_
c. I have one brother. _4_
d. Teresa has a sister. _2_
e. We are hungry. _1_

NOTES

BASIC ITALIAN
Instructions, Cultural Notes and Conversations

CAPITOLO CINQUE (5)

Gli aggettivi e la concordanza.

Most adjectives in the Italian language end in 'o' for masculine singular and in 'a' for feminine singular.

Also adjectives end in 'i' for masculine plural and in 'e' for feminine plural just like the nouns.

Basically there are three categories of adjectives: qualifying, demonstrative and possessive. Following is a list of qualifying adjectives:

Bianco (m.s.) (White)	Nero (Black)	Rosso (Red)	Giallo (Yellow)
Grigio (Gray)			
Buona (f.s.) (Good)	Ultima (Last)	Fredda (cold)	Calda (Hot)
Brutta (Ugly)			
Bianchi (1) (m.pl)	Neri	Rossi	Gialli
Grigi			
Buone (f.pl)	Ultime	Fredde	Calde
Brutte			

(1) Most words ending in **co or ca** gain an **h** in the plural to maintain the hard sound. There are some exceptions, such as the word **amico** for singular, in the plural is **amici**, but **amica** is **amiche** in the plural, it follows the rule.

The main thing to remember is that adjectives **have to agree in gender and in number with the nouns they modify** or used with. Ex: La casa e' bianca (The house is white), as it shows, the adjective agrees with the noun in gender and in singular form.

When two nouns of different gender require an adjective applicable to both, the adjective is used in the masculine plural form. Ex: Ella ha un palazzo e una villa belli (She has a beautiful building and a villa).

Additionally there are adjectives which end in 'e' for singular and in 'i' for plural. No gender is necessary with these adjectives. They can be used with either masculine or feminine nouns. Ex: Gentile or Gentili (Kind), it can be used with either gender noun, Ex: Gentile ragazza or gentile ragazzo (Kind girl or boy), Gentili ragazze or gentili ragazzi.

NOTES

The position of the adjective in a sentence depends on the context of the sentence, therefore it can precede or follow a noun, as in English.

Demonstrative adjectives indicate location in reference to things, people or animals:

Questo, masc. sing. (This)	Questi, masc. pl., (These)
Questa, fem. sing. (This)	Queste, fem. pl., (These)
Quella, fem. Sing. (That)	Quelle, fem. Pl. (Those)
Quello, masc. sing. (That) (1)	Quelli, masc. pl., (Those)
	Quegli, masc. pl. (2)
Quel, masc. (That) (1)	Quei, masc. pl., (Those) (3)

Possessive Adjectives:

For the 1st person:	sing.	mio, mia, miei, mie	(my, mine)
	plur.	nostro, nostra, nostri, nostre	(our, ours)
For the 2nd person:	sing.	tuo, tua, tuoi, tue	(your, yours)
	plur.	vostro, vostra, vostri, vostre	(your, yours)
For the 3rd person:	sing.	suo, sua, suoi, sue	(his, hers)
	plur.	loro	(their)

1. The last adjective '**loro**' remains the same for either gender or number, it never changes, it is an exception.

2. Except when referring to relatives, the definite article is always used in front of the possessive adjective, which precedes the noun. ex: Mio padre e' a casa (My father is at home) - Il mio amico e' a casa (My friend is at home.)

3. The position of the possessive adjective is usually found in front of the noun, however it could also follow the noun, depending on the context of the sentence. ex: Il tuo amico e' alto (Your friend is tall) Quel libro e' mio (That book is mine.)

4. The possessive adjective has to agree with the noun it modifies and not with subject as in English, ex: Mario sta alla sua scrivania (Mario is at his desk.) As shown 'sua' agrees with scrivania (the noun it modifies) and not the subject.

NOTES

Other Adjectives:

Bello, masc. sing.	(Beautiful) (1)	Belli, masc. pl.,	(Beautiful)
		Begli, masc. pl.,	(Beautiful) (2)
Bella, fem. sing.	(Beautiful)	Belle, fem. pl.	(Beautiful)
Bel, masc. sing.	(Beautiful) (1)	Bei, masc., pl.,	(Beautiful) (3)
Buono, masc.,	(Good) (1)	Buoni, masc. pl.,	(Good)
Buona, fem. sing.	(Good)	Buone, fem. pl.,	(Good)
Buon, masc.,	(Good) (1)		

At this point it is important to mention that, usually, no two vowels can be adjacent to one another, except when it occurs in the middle of the word. Ex. Quello amico is wrong, Quell'amico is right (That friend) - the word 'Giovanni' (Joseph) is not altered.
More on adjectives will be covered lateron in this book.

Notes: (1) These adjectives follow similar rules applying to the definite and indefinite articles, therefore:
   Quel, Bel and Buon are used in front of masculine, singular nouns: ex: Quel bambino (That child), Bel giorno (nice day), and Buon Giorno (Good Morning or Day).
   Quello, Bello and Buono are used in front of nouns which begin with s+consonant or z, pn, ps, gn. Also, these adjectives can be used after the noun: ex: Quello studente (that student) or questo giorno e' bello (this day is beautiful).

(2) The adjectives Quegli and Begli are used in front of masculine, plural nouns that begin with a vowel and in front of nouns that begin with s+consonant or z, pn, ps, gn: Quegl'Italiani (Those Italians), Begli Stati (Beautiful States), Begli Zii (Nice Uncles).

(3) Quei and Bei are used in front of masculine, plural nouns: Quei fiori (Those flowers), Bei fiori (Beautiful flowers).

Practice reading the following sentences, focusing on the adjectives:

Il vino e' bianco	(The wine is white)	Questa cosa e' brutta	(This thing is ugly)
Io ho il vino rosso	(I have the red wine)	Ascoltiamo la buona musica	(We listen to the good music)
Quella casa e' gialla	(That house is yellow)	Quel fratello e' fuori	(That brother is out)
Oggi e' un bel giorno	(Today is a nice day)	I bei fiori	(The beautiful flowers)

NOTES

BASIC ITALIAN
Instructions, Cultural Notes and Conversations

Questa casa e' fredda (This house is cold)   Questo quadro e' bello (This picture is pretty)

Queste sedie sono brutte (These chairs are ugly)   Quegli uomini sono miei parenti
(Those men are my relatives)

Quel ragazzo e' buono   (That boy is good)   Quei bambini (Those children)

Questo latte e' caldo   (This milk is hot)   Questo caffe' e' buono (This coffee is good)

Quell'ultimo giorno   (That last day)   Io sento una bella canzone
(I hear a beautiful song)

La mia famiglia e' grande. (My family is large) Il tuo libro e' interessante
(Your book is interesting)

Il mio libro e' interessante. (My book is interesting) I miei libri sono interessanti.
(My books are interesting)

Vocabulary:

Giorno	- (Day)	Stagione	- (Season)	Lunedi'	- (Monday)
Sera	- (Evening)	Primavera	- (Spring)	Martedi'	- (Tuesday)
Mattina	- (Morning)	Estate	- (Summer)	Mercoledi'	- (Wednesday)
Pomeriggio	- (Afternoon)	Autunno	- (Fall)	Giovedi'	- (Thursday)
Notte	- (Night)	Inverno	- (Winter)	Venerdi'	- (Friday)
Domani	- (Tomorrow)	Ieri	- (Yesterday)	Sabato	- (Saturday)
Settimana	- (week)	Anno	- (Year)	Domenica	- (Sunday)

Exercise 6:

Indicare il plurale dei seguenti aggettivi (Indicate the plural of the following adjectives):

1. Gentile (Kind)
2. Indipendente (Independent)
3. Notevole (Noticeable)
4. Piacevole (Pleasant)
5. Amichevole (Friendly)
11. Questa (This)
12. Quella (That)
13. Bella (Beautiful)
14. Buona (Good)
15. Cattiva (Bad)

NOTES

6. Bello (Beautiful)
7. Buono (Good)
8. Cattivo (Bad)
9. Brutto (Ugly)
10. Ultimo (last)
16. Brutta (Ugly)
17. Dolce (Sweet)
18. Fresco (Chilly)
19. Freddo (Cold)
20. Azzurra (Blue)

Exercise 7:
Place any adjective from the list in exercise 6 with each of the first ten (10) nouns from the vocabulary list above.

NOTES

BASIC ITALIAN
Instructions, Cultural Notes and Conversations

CAPITOLO SEI (6)

Gli Italiani.

This chapter will consist of some cultural notes and conversations for practical purposes.

When Italians get together there is, usually, good food, good wine and good conversation. At times the conversation appears to be intense and argumentative, but it is only indicative of the attitude and personality of the average Italian and even if tension is present, it is quickly dismissed, forgotten and laughter is soon restored. The Italians are outgoing, not shy, friendly and always willing to celebrate any occasion with processions, parties, festivals. They love to entertain. Most Italians have strong feelings of family responsibilities, as well as religious convictions.

Italian people love music and often sing by themselves or following a song being played on the radio. It is not uncommon to walk down any street, in Italy, and hear a song on the radio through the open windows or balconies and a passerby will, most likely, pick up the tune and sing along. It is very easy to strike a conversation among two Italians, who never met before, while waiting for public transportation or anywhere.

During the warm weather most coffee shops put their tables and chairs outdoors and often they are full of people. This is true, throughout Italy, from the 'Galleria' in Milan, or Piazza della Signoria in Florence, or Via Appia or Piazza di Spagna in Rome to the waterfront of Naples and Salerno, to name a few. Italians like to go walking, window shopping and then sit at an outdoor cafe' for an espresso or cappuccino or bibita (beverage). The walking has become so popular that it acquired a name of its own, 'Struscio', meaning leisure walking, often done on weekends or nights after work and before cena (supper).

The family meal is a very important part of Italian life. The main meal (Pranzo) takes place around one or two p.m. every day including weekends. At this time most offices and stores close (usually from 1 to 3 or 4 p.m.) so that the employees can go home to eat. Naturally those offices and stores will also stay open till 8 p.m. to make up the hours. Recently in the cities where there are a lot of tourists, such as Florence, Rome and others some stores do not close in the afternoon for fear of losing the tourists business and therefore place a sign in the window which says 'Orario Continuo' (Continuous hours).

Il pranzo often consists of three courses, the first being a pasta dish or soup and is served by itself. The second course will have meat or fish with a couple of side dishes, such as eggplant or potatoes, etc, with salad, and plenty of bread, wine and water, often mineral water. Sometimes a platter of a variety of cheeses may be served before the last course which is fresh fruit or, on special occasions, a cake or store bought individual pastries. After each course the plates are retrieved and replaced with clean ones.

NOTES

In the evening there is supper (Cena), which, normally is a lighter meal. Sometimes it includes leftovers, or soup and salad, cheeses, vegetables and a variety of lunch meats, but always on the light side. Of course if there are guests involved, then the Cena becomes more elaborate.

Usually each of these meals lasts one hour or two to consume so that snacking between meals, virtually, does not exist. It is during these meals that the family spends time together and shares the day's events. It is not a good idea to be late for one of these family dinners. Most Italians consider being on time for a family dinner almost as important as being at work on time. Usually on Sundays and other holidays is the time that relatives or friends join in the festivities, therefore the number of courses of the meals increases and so does the variety of foods. Buon Appetito.

Pratice reading aloud the following conversation:

Basic Italian Conversation:

Mario and Teresa are in a restaurant called 'Il Gatto Nero' (The black cat) in Venice.

Topic: Ordering regional food

Cameriere (waiter):	Buona sera, prego (Good evening, welcome)
Mario:	Un tavolo per due, per piacere (A table for two, please)
Cameriere:	Vogliono sedersi vicino alla finestra or fuori sul terrazzo? (Would like to sit near the window or outside on the patio?)
Mario:	Sul terrazzo. (on the patio)
Cameriere:	Sono Americani, vero? Che cosa desiderano prendere? (Are you Americans? What would you like to order?)
Mario:	Non sappiamo. Dov'e il menu' (We don't know, do you have the menu')
Cameriere:	Torno subito, mi scusino. (I'll be right back, excuse me)
Mario to Teresa:	Su cara, che cosa prendiamo? (Come on, Dear, what shall we have?)
Teresa:	Non lo so, Cameriere, scusi, mi puo' suggerire un bel piatto veneto? (I don't know, Waiter, excuse me, can you suggest a local dish?)
Cameriere:	Certamente, guardi che cosa le piace? (Certainly, what type of food do you like?)

NOTES

Teresa:	Mi piace antipasto caldo con formaggio e funghi. (I like an appetizer cooked with cheese and mushrooms.)
Cameriere:	Va bene. E Lei, Signore, che cosa desidera? (Fine and you, Sir, what would you like?)
Mario:	Un bel piatto di spaghetti aglio e olio. (A nice dish of spaghetti with garlic and oil)
Cameriere:	Va bene, ma questo non e' un piatto veneto. (Fine, but this is not a local dish.)
Teresa:	Ma qual'e' la specialita' della casa? (But what is the house specialty??)
Cameriere:	Il risotto e' la specialita' della casa. Ma per primo posso suggerire un bel brodetto e per secondo il risotto che e' la specialita' della casa. (Risotto is the specialty of the house. But for the first course I would suggest soup and then the risotto.)
Mario e Teresa:	Magnifico (Excellent)
Cameriere:	Che cosa bevono? Una bottiglia di acqua minerale? (What will you have to drink, a bottle of mineral water?
Mario:	Si, ma ci porti anche il vino (Yes, but bring us some wine also.)
Teresa:	Una bella bottiglia di 'Pinot Grigio"
Cameriere:	Buon Appetito. (Enjoy.)

Sotto voce Mario dice a Teresa: 'Speriamo sia tutto buono, come dice il cameriere"
(Whispering Mario says to Teresa: 'Let's hope it is all good, like the waiter says.)

NOTES

CAPITOLO SETTE (7)

La coniugazione del verbo 'Stare'
e l'uso dei pronomi 'tu' 'voi' 'Lei'.

Stare = To be or to stay					
		Present Tense			
Io	sto	(I am or stay)	noi	stiamo	(we are or stay)
Tu	stai	(you are or stay)	voi	state	(you, pl. are or stay)
lui, lei	sta	(he or she is or stays)	loro	stanno	(they are or stay)

This verb, when used to mean 'to stay' is considered a regular verb, but when it is used to mean 'to be' then, is considered a helping verb and used with other verbs as well as by itself. 'Stare' verb is frequently used when people greet each other.

The following samples will show the variety of uses of the verb 'Stare'.

Oggi io sto a casa (Today I stay home) -

Tu stai fuori (You stay outside) -

Noi stiamo in giardino (We are in the garden)

Come stai? (How are you?)

Sto bene, grazie (I am fine, thanks) -

Come sta tua madre? (How is your mother?)

Che stai facendo (what are you doing) -

Che stai dicendo (What are you saying) -

Dove stai andando - (where are you going)

Note that in the last three samples, the verb **stare** functions as a helping verb, more on this topic later on.

A few notes: The verb 'stare' is interchangeable, in its use, with the verb 'essere'. At times it will be clear which one fits a sentence better and other times it is appropriate to use either one in a particular sentence, without changing the meaning of the sentence. Only practice will help. There are rules but are long and complex with many exceptions, therefore, for the purpose of this book, simplification is preferred.

NOTES

Another point to mention is that often, in the Italian language, the auxiliary verb used, is the opposite of what is used in english, ex: Sono stato (have been); Quanti anni hai? (How old are you?).

Interrogative or Negative:

To form the interrogative in any verb, the structure of the sentence does not have to change. It simply requires a question mark in writing or an inflection of the voice, when speaking, to indicate the question. To form a negative in any verb, simply add '**non**' (not) in front of the verb used. Double negative does exist in Italian, therefore it is proper to say 'noi non abbiamo niente' (we don't have nothing - **literally** -) or (we don't have anything.)

A word of caution: it is very difficult to translate literally, often it results in a totally different meaning or inappropriate grammar use as the double negative sentence shows above. It is recommended and preferable that the Italian structure is learned for conversation purposes.

The use of the pronouns 'tu', 'voi', 'lei':

The pronoun '**tu**' is used referring to friends, relatives, peers and children, in the singular form, meaning talking to one person only or writing. With this pronoun the required verb is always the **second person singular** in any tense, ex: Tu hai una mela (You have an apple).

The pronoun '**voi**' is used referring to two or more people and the **second person plural** of any verb is the correct form of the verb to be used, ex: Voi avete ragione (You, pl, are right).
This pronoun can be used also when referring to one person, to whom one wants to show respect, or to a person of authority, ex: Don Giovanni, voi come state? (Don Giovanni, how are you?)

The pronoun '**Lei**' is used referring to a person, masculine or feminine, to whom one wants to show respect by using a polite or formal way of addressing a person, both in talking or writing. This formal way is used frequently in stores, offices, banks, where normally people do not know each other. When using this pronoun the **third person singular** of any verb is necessary, ex: Lei come sta oggi? (How are you today?).

History note: The Romans did not bother with all these formalities, they used the very familiar pronoun 'tu' talking with anybody, whether it was the emperor or the slave. Today these formalities are very much observed throughout Italy.

NOTES

Practice reading along the following sentences, focusing on the verbs:

Io sto bene	(I am fine)	Lui sta in giardino	(He is in the garden)
Io sto a casa	(I am at home)	Noi stiamo in macchina	(We are in the car)
Io sono a casa	(I am at home)	Loro stanno fuori	(They are out)
Lei come sta?	(How are you?)	Loro stanno qui in estate	(They are here in the summer)
Tu stai male?	(Are you not feeling well?)	Quei fiori sono qui	(Those flowers are here)

Un bel viaggio e' andare in Italia   (A nice trip is to go to Italy)

Mercoledi' e' il principio d'estate   (Wednesday is the beginning of the summer)

Lunedi' stiamo in treno per andare a Milano   (Monday we are on the train to go to Milan)

D'inverno fa freddo in Nord Italia   (In the winter it is cold in North Italy)

Questi bambini stanno a casa della Nonna   (These children stay at the home of the Grandmother)

Tu stai a casa di amici?   (Are you staying at friends' house?)

La primavera e' una bella stagione   (The spring is a beautiful season)

Il vino rosso sta a tavola   (The red wine is on the table)

L'acqua e i bicchieri sono a tavola   (The water and the glasses are on the table)

L'acqua e i bicchieri stanno a tavola   (The water and the glasses are on the table)

Vocabulary:

E	- (and)	Tazza	- (Cup)	Forchetta	-	(Fork)
E'	- (Is)	Tazzina	- (Little cup)	Forchettina	-	(Little fork)
Tovaglia	- (Tablecloth)	Piattino	- (Small dish)	Coltello	-	(Knife)

NOTES

Tovagliolino - (Napkin)   Cucchiaio - (Spoon)   Coltellino - (Little knife)

Piatto   - ((Dish))   Cucchiaino - (Teaspoon) Brocca   - (Pitcher)

Exercise 8:

Describe ten (10) items most likely found on a dinner table adding the definite article to them.

Exercise 9:

Conjugate the verbs 'Stare' - 'Essere' - 'Avere' (present tense)

NOTES

BASIC ITALIAN
Instructions, Cultural Notes and Conversations

CAPITOLO OTTO (8)

Una visita a Siena (A visit to Siena).

Siena is a beautiful, old, medieval town and should be included in any tourist's itinerary for that region. The city is located in the Tuscany region about one hour drive south of Florence. It is a very pleasant drive from Florence to Siena, overlooking the rich fields filled with olive trees, vineyards and plenty of cypress trees on the way. Long ago Siena used to be a Roman colony and at one time Florence was its rival city. There are many beautiful and historic sights to see, including, but not limited to, the Cathedral with its magnificent paintings inside and remarkable sculptures. Among the well known ones is the Pulpit by Nicola Pisano, made in the 13th century. It is just breathtaking to look at. The Cathedral was done in the Gothic style, which was a prevalent style of architecture in the 13th century. Santa Caterina di Siena, who is the patron saint of Italy, comes from this city. The main square of Siena, Piazza del Campo is internationally known. It is a very large square, with very old, but attractive buildings around it, with its many openings leading to the small, narrow, charming cobblestone streets, lined with stores, churches, museums etc. Piazza del Campo is the center of town and in it, takes place one of the most unique and characteristic festivals, every year, where people, from many places, come to see it, they call it il Palio. This summer event is a horse race sponsored by the various local districts with no strict rules and possibly anything can happen. The riders ride the horses, bareback, and are dressed in the fancy costumes with a particular color depicting their district. They run around the square, prepared with dirt ahead of time, three times. This festival was originally started to honor the 'Madonna di Provenzano' and therefore it starts with a procession, and the blessing. The procession includes the flag bearers with their different colors from each sponsoring district. From the balconies of the buildings surrounding the square, people display the flags of the district they are rooting for, and when the procession is complete and all the horses show up in the square, the race is on. The atmosphere during the preparations for this event and during the festivities is really exciting. It is a great honor to be able to win the race and naturally the winner is held in high esteem by the local people.

Following is the translation of above paragraphs into Italian for the purpose of reading, understanding and practice the pronunciation as well as the structure of the sentences.

Traduzione di una visita a Siena: (Translation of a visit to Siena)

Siena e' una citta' bella, vecchia, medievale e dovrebbe essere inclusa nell'itinerario di ogni turista di questa regione. La citta' e' nella regione toscana, circa un'ora al sud di Firenze. E' una bella passeggiata in macchina da Firenze a Siena, durante la guida si vedono i bei campi pieni di alberi di olive, vigneti e molti alberi di cipressi. Molto tempo fa Siena era una colonia Romana ed una volta Firenze era la citta' rivale di Siena. Ci sono molti posti belli ed istorici da vedere, incluso, ma non solo, la Cattedrale coi magnifici quadri e le sculture eccezionali. Tra i piu' famosi e' il Pulpito, fatto da Nicola Pisano, nel tredicesimo secolo. E' magnifico a vedere. La Cattedrale e' stata fatta nello stile Gotico, il quale era lo stile prevalente nel tredicesimo secolo. Santa Caterina di Siena, che e' la santa

NOTES

BASIC ITALIAN
Instructions, Cultural Notes and Conversations

protettrice d'Italia, originalmente era di Siena. La piazza principale di Siena e' Piazza del Campo ed e' famosa internazionalmente. E' una piazza molto grande con molti palazzi vecchi e caratteristici, e con molte aperture che danno sulle stradine che sono piccole, strette e incantevoli, lineate con i negozi, chiese, musei ecc. La piazza e' il centro della citta' e in questa piazza accade, ogni anno, uno dei piu' unici e caratteristici festival, dove la gente viene dappertutto, si chiama il Palio. Quest'evento estivo si trattra di una corsa di cavalli, promossa da varie contrade locali con poche regole e quindi ogni cosa puo' succedere. I cavalieri vanno sui cavalli senza sella e sono vestiti con costumi di tempi antichi con un particolare colore che appartiene alla contrada che rappresentano. Corrono intorno alla piazza tre volte, la piazza e' precedentemente preparata per cavalcare. Questo festival originalmente comincio' per onorare la 'Madonna di Provenzano' e quindi oggi le festivita' cominciano con una processione e la benedizione. La processione include i portatori di bandiere di diversi colori rappresentando le varie contrade. Dai balconi dei palazzi intorno alla piazza, la gente mette fuori le bandiere della contrada favorita e quando la processione e' completa e tutti i cavalli sono in Piazza, la corsa comincia. L'atmosfera, durante le preparazioni per questo evento e durante le festivita', e' molto eccitante. E' un grande onore essere capace di vincere la corsa e naturalmente il vincitore e' tenuto in alta stima dalla gente locale.

For practice in this chapter try to analyze the Italian paragraphs above and determine the components of the grammar, covered so far, such as adjectives, verbs, definite and indefinite articles, tenses of verbs (infinitive and present tense).

1. Underline all the adjectives in the first paragraph of Italian version above.

2. Find the definite and indefinite articles in the same paragraph of the Italian version above.

3. Insert the answer to the following sentences:

    a. In quale regione e' Siena? _____

    b. Come si chiama il festival di Siena?_____

    c. In macchina da Firenze a Siena che si vede_____

    d. La piazza del Campo e' piccola? _____

    e. Quanto tempo dista Siena da Firenze _____

    f. Quali sono le prime due cose che fanno al principio del festival?

    _____

NOTES

BASIC ITALIAN
Instructions, Cultural Notes and Conversations

Two tourists in Florence discuss whether or not to go to Siena, and then they decide to go.

Caterina:	Ci sono molti posti belli da vedere, andiamo a Siena? (There are many beautiful places to see, shall we go to Siena?)
Giovanni:	Chissa' quanto tempo ci vuole per guidare da qui? (Who knows how long it takes to drive from here?)
Caterina:	Penso un'ora di macchina, andiamo? (I think 1 hour by car, let's go?)
Giovanni:	Ma sai niente di Siena? (But do you know anything about Siena?)
Caterina:	Non personalmente, ma ho parlato con alcune persone dell'albergo, che sono stati a Siena e dicono che, senza dubbio, si deve visitare. E' un posto bello ed interessante. (Not personally, but I have spoken with some people from the hotel, who have been to Siena and they said that, without a doubt, it must be visited. It is a beautiful and interesting place.)
Giovanni:	Allora affittiamo una macchina e andiamo. (Well, then let's rent a car and let's go.)
Caterina:	Va bene, vado a telefonare per una macchina. (OK, I am going to phone for a car)
Giovanni:	Questa macchina va bene, le strade sono piccole e curve. (This car drives ok, the streets are small and curvy.)
Caterina:	Si, certo, ma il paesaggio e' bello, vedi quei vigneti, sono alti, e gli alberi, e' una bella passeggiata. (Yes, sure, but the landscape is beautiful, see those vineyards, they are tall, and the trees, it is a nice drive.)
Giovanni:	Si, certo, e' una bella passeggiata, ma devo guardare la strada per il traffico. (Yes, sure, it is a nice drive, but I must look the street for the traffic.)
Caterina:	Ecco, finalmente arriviamo a Siena. (Here, we finally arrive in Siena.)
Giovanni:	Parcheggiamo la macchina e andiamo a trovare un ristorante e un albergo. (Let's park the car and then we go to look for a restaurant and a hotel)
Caterina:	Si, va bene, ho anch'io appetito. (Yes, Ok, I am hungry too)

NOTES

Giovanni:	Prima di andare al ristorante, troviamo un negozio e compriamo un libro di Siena, cosi possiamo leggere circa i posti per visitare mentre aspettiamo per essere serviti. (Before we go to the restaurant, let's find a bookstore and buy a book on Siena, so we can read about places to see while we wait to eat)
Caterina:	Benissimo, che buona idea hai. (Great, what a good idea you have)
Giovanni:	Sto leggendo il libro di Siena e vedo che possiamo cominciare a Piazza del Campo e dopo la Cattedrale. (I am reading the book about Siena and I see that we can start at Piazza del Campo and afterward the Cathedral)
Caterina:	D'accordo, ma desidero vedere anche i negozi dopo o forse domani. (Agreed, but I wish to see, also, the stores afterward or maybe tomorrow)
Giovanni:	Si, certo. (Yes, sure)
Caterina:	Cerchiamo di trovare un albergo vicino a Piazza del Campo, cosi non dobbiamo camminare molto. (Let's try to find a hotel near the Piazza del Campo, so that we don't have to walk a lot)
Giovanni	Ma Siena non e' grande, quindi tutto e' relativamente vicino in citta'. (But Siena is not big, so that everything is relatively close in town)
Caterina:	Si, hai ragione. (Yes, you are right)
Giovanni:	Ecco, Piazza del Campo, come e' bella, vero? Vedi quei palazzi, sono molto vecchi, ma sono ancora molto belli e caratteristici dell'epoca. (Here, Piazza del Campo, how beautiful it is, true? See those buildings, they are very old, but they are still very pretty and caratheristic of the era)
Caterina:	Si, e' vero, la Piazza e' molto bella e anche i palazzi. Vedi quella fontana, andiamo piu' vicino; la fontana non e' molto grande, e' rettangolare, ma ha molte statue. Il libro spiega che queste statue sono repliche e le originali sono nel museo. (Yes, it's true, the Piazza is beautiful and also the buildings. See that fountain, let's go closer, the fountain is not very big, rectangular, but it has many statues. The book says these are copies, the originals are in the museum)

NOTES

Giovanni:	E' bene che hanno buona cura delle statue, perche' eventualmente si rovinano fuori. (It is good that they preserve these statues, because, eventually, they would be destroyed outside)
Caterina:	Sei pronto per andare a vedere la Cattedrale? Dista solo pochi minuti da qui (Are you ready to go see the Cathedral? It is only a few minutes from here)
Giovanni:	D'accordo, andiamo. (OK, let's go)
Caterina:	C'e' tanto da vedere, da dove cominciamo? (There is much to see, where shall we start?)
Giovanni:	Seguiamo la guida nel libro, vedi quante cappelle con statue a sinistra e anche a destra ci sono. Il libro spiega che nella cappella di San Giovanni Battista, c'e' una grande statua di bronzo del Battista, andiamo a vedere. (Let's follow the book guide, see how many chapels with statues there are both to the left and also to the right. The book explains that in the chapel of Saint John the Baptist, there a large statue of bronze of the Baptist, let's go see it)
Caterina:	Ecco, la cappella ma la statua non c'e', il cartello spiega che e' in ristorazione. Nota anche i pavimenti di mosaici, sono pieni di colori con scene dalla Bibbia. (Here is the chapel but the statue is not here, the sign explains that the statue is out for restoration work. Notice mosaic floors, they are full of colors with scenes from the Bible)
Giovanni:	Vedi che alcune zone di pavimenti di mosaici hanno i cordoni attorno perche' con tanti turisti e col passare del tempo i pavimenti si rovinano. Bisogna preservarli. (See that some areas of the mosaic floors have ropes around them so to keep poeple off, because with so many tourists and with the passage of time the floors will be destroyed. They must be preserved)
Caterina:	Un giorno dobbiamo tornare a vedere, di nuovo, tanti capolavori d'arte. (Some day we must return to see, again, all these masterpieces of art)
Giovanni:	Si, hai ragione, c' difficile assorbire tanta storia e cultura in una sola visita, torneremo. (Yes, you are right, it is difficult to absorb so much history and culture in only one visit, we will come back)

NOTES

BASIC ITALIAN
Instructions, Cultural Notes and Conversations

Vocabulary: I mesi dell'anno: (the months of the year)

Mese	-	(Month)	Gennaio	- (January)	Luglio	- (July)
Anno	-	(Year)	Febbraio	- (February)	Agosto	- (August)
			Marzo	- (March)	Settembre	- (September)
			Aprile	- (April)	Ottobre	- (October)
			Maggio	- (May)	Novembre	- (November)
			Giugno	- (June)	Dicembre	- (December)

NOTES

BASIC ITALIAN
Instructions, Cultural Notes and Conversations

CAPITOLO NOVE (9)

Le preposizioni.

Dalle finestre **della** casa **della** sua famiglia, la ragazza poteva vedere la strada, specialmente l'angolo **della** strada dove l'amico la veniva a prendere **di** Domenica **sulla** motocicletta. La casa era sul terzo piano e cosi come la ragazza vedeva l'amico, salutava tutti **in** famiglia e scendeva per incontrare il suo amico.

From the windows of her family's house, the girl could see the street and especially the corner of the street where her boyfriend would come to pick her up every Sunday on the motorcycle. The house was on the third floor and so, as the girl saw her friend, she would say goodbye to all in the family and would come down to meet with him.

Prepositions:

There are, basically, two types of prepositions which will be covered in this chapter. The simple prepositions and those combined with the article. Prepositions, in Italian, are not only used in front of nouns, but also sometimes in front of verbs as it will be shown lateron.

The simple prepositions are:

    di (of or from)   **da (from or by)**   **a (to or at)**   **in (in)**

    con (with)   **su (on)**   **per (per)**   **tra or fra (among)**

The prepositions when combined with the appropriate definite article have the following forms:

(The definite article= il - l' - lo - la - i - gli - le)

NOTES

> di + article   = del, dello, della, dei, degli, delle   (of the)
>
> da + article   = dal, dallo, dalla, dai, dagli, dalle   (from the)
>
> a + article   = al, allo, alla, ai, agli, alle   (to the or at the)
>
> in + article   = nel, nello, nella, nei, negli, nelle   (in the)
>
> con + article = col, coi (only in the masculine, it is not combined when used with a feminine noun) -
>
> su + article   = sul, sullo, sulla, sui, sugli, sulle   (on the)

Notes: 1. The prepositions **per, tra or fra** are never combined with the article. 2. The above combined prepositions do follow the same rules of the definite articles.

Examples: Spero **di** venire (I hope to come) - **Da** dove vieni? (From where are you coming?)

Di dove sei? (Where are you from?) - Oggi mangio **a** casa (Today I eat at home)

Oggi sto **in** citta' (Today I stay in town) - Io sto in citta' **con** Maria (I am in town with Maria) -

Il colore **del** fiore (The color of the flower) - Il libro **dello** studente (The student's book) -

Il libro **della** studentessa (The book of - Il numero **degli** spettacoli (The number the student, fem.)   of the shows)

Gli spaghetti **al** dente   (The spaghetti to the tooth, not overcooked) -

Maria e' **coi** ragazzi   (Maria is with the boys).

More on Verbs and the introduction of the Past Participle:

As explained in the third chapter, verbs end in **are/ere/ire** in the infinitive tense. This is the way they are listed in the dictionary. The stem of the verb is, usually, present in all the conjugation of that verb. To determine the stem, simply delete the are/ere/or ire endings and add the appropriate ending for a particular tense, for now it is the present tense. Previously covered is the verb ASCOLTARE - the stem is **ASCOLT** -

NOTES

Taking the same concept and applying it to another **are** verb, we have the following:

Mangiare		(To eat)		
io	mangio	(I eat)	noi mangiamo	(we eat)
tu	mangi	(you eat)	voi mangiate	(you, pl. eat)
lui, lei	mangia	(he or she eats)	loro mangiano	(they eat)

Notes: 1. When there are two 'i', one in the stem ot the verb and the other in the ending of the second person singular, usually, one 'i' is deleted as seen in 'mangi' above.- 2. By learning to determine the stem of any regular verb and the endings of the present tense, a student should be able to conjugate any verb.

Past Participle:

This verb form is used primarily with the auxiliary verbs 'essere or avere' (to be or to have). To form the past participle of any regular verb ending in **are/ere/ire**, again, simply remove are/ere/ire and replace it with **ato/uto/ito.**

Examples:	ascoltare	= ascolt**ato**	(listened)	-mangiare	= mangi**ato**	(eaten)
	parlare	= parl**ato**	(spoken)	-cantare	= cant**ato**	(sung)
	vendere	= vend**uto**	(sold)	-mantenere	= manten**uto**	(kept)
	sentire	= sent**ito**	(heard)	-partire	= part**ito**	(left)

Note: 1. The conjugation of Italian verbs is very different from the conjugation of English verbs. Some tenses in the Italian verbs do not exist in the English verbs. Other tenses do not correspond with those in English.
The usage of the tenses in Italian verbs is also very different than in the English language. Names of tenses will be used in order to identify the verbs, however studying the various examples given in this book will help. Example: Ieri ho scritto (past participle) una lettera (yesterday I wrote a letter).

If the sentence was written in the following way: Scrissi (past tense) una lettera (I wrote a letter), that would indicate the action took place long ago, not recently.

NOTES

Practice reading aloud the following sentences:

Io ho ascoltato la radio	(I have listened to the radio)
Io ho ascoltato la maestra.	(I have listened to the teacher)
Tu hai parlato in inglese.	(You have spoken in english)
Lui ha venduto una casa.	(He has sold a house)
Noi abbiamo sentito un rumore	(We have heard a noise)
Voi avete mangiato una mela	(You, pl., have eaten an apple)
Essi hanno cantato una bella canzone	(They have sung a beautiful song)
Io sono partito per la citta'	(I have left for the town)
Tu sei andato in citta'	(You have gone to town)
Lei e' arrivata a casa	(She has arrived at home)
Noi siamo partiti col treno	(We have left with the train)
Voi siete andati a casa	(You have gone to the house)
Esse sono partite in macchina	(They, fem., have left by car)

Notes:
1. As a general rule of thumb when using the verb 'essere', as a helping verb, the past participle, usually, agrees with the subject.

2. When the gender is not specified or there is mixed gender, the masculine will be used.

3. Notice that often when in english the verb 'to have' is used, in Italian the verb' to be' is used instead, as shown above.

Vocabulary:

Partire	-	To leave	Treno	-	Train	Biglietto	- Ticket
Arrivare	-	To arrive	Aeroplano	-	Airplane	Sedile	- Seat

NOTES

Cantare	-	To sing	Canzone	-	Song	Bella	-	Beautiful
Sentire	-	To hear	Rumore	-	Noise	Strano	-	Strange
Mangiare	-	To eat	Torta	-	Cake	Buona	-	Good

Exercise 10:

Place the prepositions combined with the appropriate article to the following sentences:

1. I colori _____ fiori sono brillanti. (The colors of the flowers are shining).

2. I biscotti _____ caffe' sono buoni. (The cookies with the coffee are good)

3. Le mele _____ mercato sono fresche. (The apples of the market are fresh)

4. La sorella _____ studente si chiama Maria. (The student's sister's name is Maria)

5. Il padre _____ bambina e' in ufficio (The father of the child is in the office)

6. A casa _____ studenti ci sono libri. (There are books at the house of the students)

7. Andiamo _____ cinema oggi? (Are we going to the movies today?)

8. Le mele sono _____ cestino (The apples are in the basket)

9. La penna e' _____ scrivania (The pen is on the desk)

10. Vedo la macchina _____ finestra (I see the car from the window)

Practice reading the following paragraph:

Al ritorno dalla scuola, la madre chiede alla figlia 'che cosa hai fatto a scuola oggi?' La figlia risponde: 'ho ascoltato la maestra e ho fatto i compiti per domani. Abbiamo mangiato una buona colezione' la figlia continua 'nel pomeriggio abbiamo parlato di storia e poi siamo andati a casa.'

On returning from school, the mother asks the daughter 'what have you done in school today?' The daughter answers: 'I have listened to the teacher and I have done the homework for tomorrow. Then we had a good lunch' the daughter continues 'in the afternoon we talked about history and then we went home.

NOTES

BASIC ITALIAN
Instructions, Cultural Notes and Conversations

CAPITOLO DIECI (10)

I comparativi degli aggettivi.

In un piccolo paese in Nord Italia, c'erano due ragazzi che andavano in bicicletta. Erano fratelli, si chiamavano Mario e Giuseppe. Giuseppe era **piu' grande** di Mario. I ragazzi andavano al negozio per comprare il pane per la madre. Arrivati al negozio Mario prende una pagnotta di pane e dice al fratello, 'compriamo questa?' il fratello dice 'no, compriamo quest'altra, che e' non solo **piu' buona** della tua ma e' **buonissima.**'

In a little town in north Italy, there were two boys who were going on bicycles. They were brothers and their names were Mario & Giuseppe. Giuseppe was older than Mario. The boys were going to the store to buy some bread for their mother. Once in the store, Mario picks up a loaf of bread and asks his brother 'shall we buy this one' the brother says 'no, let's buys this other kind, which is, not only, better than that. but it is very, very good.

Comparisons of adjectives:

Positive		Comparative		Superlative	
Grande	(big)	Piu' grande	(bigger)	Grandissimo	(biggest)
Bravo	(capable)	Piu' bravo	(more capable)	Bravissimo	(most capable)
Bello	(beautiful)	Piu' bello	(more beautiful)	Bellissimo	(most beautiful)
Piccolo	(little)	Piu' piccolo	(littler)	Piccolissimo	(littlest)
Basso	(short)	Piu' basso	(shorter)	Bassissimo	(shortest)
Alto	(tall)	Piu' alto	(taller)	Altissimo	(tallest)
Caro	(dear)	Piu' caro	(dearer)	Carissimo	(dearest)
Bianco	(white)	Piu' bianco	(whiter)	Bianchissimo	(whitest)
Nero	(black)	Piu' nero	(blacker)	Nerissimo	(blackest)

NOTES

Azzurro   (blue)   Piu' azzurro   (bluer)   Azzurrissimo   (bluest)

Irregular Comparatives and Superlatives:

Positive	Comparative	Superlative Absolute	Superlative Relative
Buono	Piu' buono or migliore	Buonissimo or Ottimo	Il piu' buono or il migliore
Cattivo	Piu' cattivo or Peggiore	Cattivissimo o Pessimo ---	Il piu' cattivo or Il peggiore
Grande	Piu' grande or Maggiore	Grandissimo or Massimo ---	Il piu' grande or Il maggiore
Piccolo	Piu' piccolo or minore	Piccolissimo or minimo	Il piu' piccolo

Practice reading the following sentences:

La casa e' piccolissima.	(The house is smallest or very small)
Il mio caffe' e' piu' buono di ieri.	(My coffee is better than yesterday)
Questa casa e' grandissima	(This house is biggest or very big)
La mela e' piu' buona della pera.	(The apple is better than the pear)
Oggi le mele sono buonissime	(Today the apples are best)
La ragazza e' brava.	(The girl is capable or skilled)
La sua gatta e' grande	(Her cat is big)
La finestra e' piu' alta.	(The window is higher)
Il loro pranzo e' buono	(Their dinner is good)
I piatti sono bellissimi	(The dishes are beautiful)
La macchina fotografica e' piccola.	(The camera is small)

NOTES

Il portafoglio e' piu' piccolo. (The wallet is smaller)

Vostro padre e' alto. (Your father is tall)

Il mio gatto e' piu' grande del tuo (My cat is bigger than yours)

Il mio giardino e' grandissimo (My garden is very big)

Il mio giardino e' il piu grande del vicinato (My garden is the biggest of the neighbourhood)

Oggi il cielo e' azzurrissimo (Today the sky is very blue)

La signora ha tre figli, il maggiore ha dieci anni (The lady has three sons, the oldest is 10)

Questo pranzo e' ottimo (This dinner is excellent)

Mario e' piu' alto di Giovanni (Mario is taller than Giovanni)

Vocabulary:

Figlio -	(Son)	Cugino -	(Cousin)	Nonno -	(Grandfather)
Figlia -	(Daughter)	Suocera -	(Mother-in-law)	Nonna -	(Grandmother)
Padre -	(Father)	Suocero -	(Father-in-law)	Genitori -	(Parents)
Madre -	(Mother)	Nipote -	(Nephew)	Parenti -	(Relatives)
Sorella -	(Sister)	Nuora -	(Daughter-in-law)	Zio -	(Uncle)
Fratello -	(Brother)	Genero -	(Son-in-law)	Zia -	(Aunt)

Exercise 11: Tradurre le frasi seguenti:

1. My pen is on the desk.
2. Maria's father is taller than Mario's father.
3. My house is beautiful.
4. Your house is big.
5. His office has a window.
6. My brother speaks Italian.
7. My books are on the desk
8. Their car is little.
9. The prices are highest or dearest.
10. This wine is better than that wine.

NOTES

BASIC ITALIAN
Instructions, Cultural Notes and Conversations

Exercise 12: Completare le frasi seguenti:

1. Il mio cane e' _____(bigger) del tuo gatto.

2. La signora Esposito ha tre figli, _____(the littlest) ha tre anni.

3. L'opera, La Traviata, e' _____(most beautiful) e la soprano e' _____(most capable).

4. Il _____(your, pl) giardino e' _____(big).

5. Michele e' _____(shorter) di Giovanni.

6. Oggi il cielo e' _____(bluer) di ieri.

7. Questo negozio ha i prezzi_____(dearer) di quell'altro negozio.

8. Il ponte vecchio in Firenze e' _____(little), ma famoso.

9. Tuo padre e tua madre sono molto _____(tall).

10. I tuoi amici sono _____(bad).

NOTES

CAPITOLO UNDICI (11)

Teresa vuole andare da Firenze a Napoli col treno e dice al bigliettaio che vuole comprare un biglietto per Napoli col treno, che parte da Firenze alle **tre** di pomeriggio e arriva a Napoli alle **sette e trenta**. Il bigliettaio chiede a Teresa se vuole **prima** o **seconda** classe. Teresa dice per **prima** classe, e quanto costa? Il bigliettaio dice che costa **cento cinquanta** mila lire che sono circa **novanta** dollari a persona per andata e ritorno. Teresa dice che va bene e lo compra.

Teresa wants to go from Florence to Naples with the train and says to the clerk that she wants to buy a ticket for Naples with the train, which leaves Florence at three p.m. and arrives in Naples at seven-thirty. The clerk asks Teresa if she wants it for first or second class. Teresa says for first class, and asks how much it costs. The clerk says it costs a hundred and fifty thousand lire, which is almost ninety dollars, per person for round trip. Teresa says she will buy it.

I numeri.:

The cardinal numbers - I numeri cardinali:

1.	Uno	21.	Ventuno	50.	Cinquanta
2.	Due	22.	Ventidue	60.	Sessanta
3.	Tre	23.	Ventitre	70.	Settanta
4.	Quattro	24.	Ventiquattro	80.	Ottanta
5.	Cinque	25.	Venticinque	90.	Novanta
6.	Sei	26.	Ventisei	100.	Cento
7.	Sette	27.	Ventisette	101.	Centouno
8.	Otto	28.	Ventotto	102.	Centodue
9.	Nove	29.	Ventinove	103.	Centotre
10.	Dieci	30.	Trenta		
11.	Undici	31.	Trentuno	200.	Duecento
12.	Dodici	32.	Trentadue	300.	Trecento
13.	Tredici	33.	Trentatre	400.	Quattrocento
14.	Quattordici	34.	Trentaquattro	500.	Cinquecento
15.	Quindici	35.	Trentacinque	600.	Seicento
16.	Sedici	36.	Trentasei	700.	Settecento
17.	Diciasette	37.	Trentasette	800.	Ottocento
18.	Diciotto	38.	Trentotto	900.	Novecento
19.	Diciannove	39.	Trentanove	1000.	Mille
20.	Venti	40.	Quaranta	2000.	Duemila

NOTES

The ordinal numbers - I numeri ordinali:

1.	Primo	13.	Tredicesimo
2.	Secondo	14.	Quattordicesimo
3.	Terzo	15.	Quindicesimo
4.	Quarto	16.	Sedicesimo
5.	Quinto	17.	Diciasettesimo
6.	Sesto	18.	Diciottesimo
7.	Settimo	19.	Diciannovesimo
8.	Ottavo	20.	Ventesimo
9.	Nono	21.	Ventunesimo
10.	Decimo	22.	Ventiduesimo
11.	Undicesimo	23.	Ventitreesimo
12.	Dodicesimo	24.	Ventiquattresimo

1. The ordinal numbers have to agree in gender and number with the noun it modifies, ex: La decima persona in fila (The tenth person in line).

2. When stating a date the day is always placed before the month, ex: 20 Giugno, 1997 or 20/6/1997.

3. When pronouncing the year, the following is used, ex: 1997 -**Mille Novecento Novanta Sette.**

Time of Day:

What time is it? = Che ora e'? or Che ore sono?

Ora = Hour   Mezzogiorno = Midday   Mezzanotte = Midnight

Pomeriggio = Afternoon   Sera = Evening   Notte = Night   Mattina = Morning

1. It is necessary to place the definite article in front of the hour.

Examples: Che ora e'?   E' l'una   (What time is it - It is one o'clock).

Che ore sono? Sono le due di pomeriggio   (What time is it - It is two in the afternoon)

Che ore sono? Sono le due e mezzo   (What time is it - It is half past two)

Che ore sono? Sono le quattro meno un quarto (What is it - It is three forty five)

NOTES

Practice reading the following paragraph, focusing on the time and the numbers:

La ragazza invita l'amica a pranzo a casa di sua madre. L'amica chiede a che ora e' il pranzo. La ragazza risponde alle sei di pomeriggio. La ragazza spiega che di solito loro pranzano piu' presto, ma, quel giorno, il padre arriva alle cinque dal lavoro. La ragazza dice all'amica che lei abita al quinto piano nel terzo palazzo a Via Garibaldi venendo da Via del Campo. Arriva il giorno dell'invito e l'amica guarda l'orologio per vedere che ore sono e vede che sono le cinque e un quarto e comincia a prepararsi per andare a pranzo a casa della ragazza.

The girl invites her friend for dinner at her mother's house. The friend asks at what time is dinner. The girl answers at six. The girl explains that usually they eat earlier but, that day, her father comes home at five from work. The girl says to her friend that she lives on the fifth floor in the third building on Via Garibaldi, coming from Via del Campo. When the day of the invitation comes, the friend looks at the clock and sees that it is a quarter after five and starts to get ready to go to dinner at her friend's house.

Vocabulary:

Cambio	-	Exchange	Comprare	-	To buy
Mancia	-	Tip	Vendere	-	To sell
Cassa	-	Register	Sconto	-	Discount
Soldi	-	Money	Banca	-	Bank
Tasse	-	Taxes	Prezzo	-	Price
Resto	-	Change	Orario	-	Hours of Operation
Negozio	-	Store	Apertura	-	Opening
Chiusura	-	Closure	Chiudere	-	To close
Conto	-	Bill	Pagare	-	To pay

NOTES

Exercise 13:

Tradurre le frasi seguenti:

1. My sister lives on the first floor.
2. My brother arrives at eight o'clock at night.
3. The wine costs four thousand lire.
4. Maria has ten apples.
5. How much does this dish cost?
6. The child has three pencils.
7. At what time does the film start?
8. The film starts at seven o'clock.
9. This is the tenth lesson.
10. The hotel is expensive.

Exercise 14:

Memorize the Italian numbers one through fifteen.

NOTES

BASIC ITALIAN
Instructions, Cultural Notes and Conversations

CAPITOLO DODICI (12)

I cibi e i vini d'Italia.

The dinner time is the lifeline of the average Italian family. Stores close, offices close and many other business offices stay closed during the dinner hours, usually from 1 to 3 or 4, to allow employees to join their families for this very important major meal of the day. A great deal of preparation and planning goes into a meal and the emphasis is on freshness.

The shopping for the dinner is done daily for the most part. It is almost inconceivable to serve bread or salad greens from the day before. There are very few supermarkets, the majority of the stores sell one category of food, such as dairy products (latticini) and related items. The fresh produce and fresh fish market is available most of the time and especially during the high season of the various products. Fruit is abundant and is often the dessert for an average meal. So to accomplish the daily shopping a typical Italian housewife makes several stops at various stores, which are often located fairly near to one another.

On the average a meal begins with a pasta dish or soup, a meat or fish next with several side dishes (two minimum), salad and last, fruit or small pastries on special occasions. The first course, pasta dish, is called Primo Piatto, the meat or fish dish is called Secondo Piatto, and then the fruit. Sometimes a tray of a variety of cheeses is offered before the fruit. At each of these courses a clean plate is offered. On holidays or special occasions the number of courses increase and the meal becomes more elaborate. For example it is not unusual to have for a Easter dinner three kinds of meat, beef, lamb and poultry, not to choose a favorite kind, but to have a taste of all three. It is also common to wait a few minutes between courses, often because the second course is still being prepared. A small cup of espresso (un bel caffe') is always a nice conclusion to a nice meal for an Italian. There is always a tablecloth covering the table and, of course, plenty of wine and bread available. It is very possible that the preparation for the next meal begins shortly after the siesta (a short rest period) time is over.

La Cucina Italiana. (The Italian cooking)

Italian cooking, with its many flavors, aromas, herbs, continues to grow in its notoriety through the western world. Among the many appealing qualities of the Italian cooking, the olive oil, grains, fresh vegetables, herbs, fish, cheeses, fruit, wines and breads prevail in making the Italian cooking a favorite with many people.

Italian merchants have been exporting pasta, olive oil and cheeses for many years, therefore several items and their origin are well known, such as Parmigiano Reggiano (from Parma). The Italian cooking varies from region to region and from town to town. There is so much diversification in the Cucina Italiana, with each region specializing in its unique type of food and style of cooking, that there is no room for any other type of cooking.

NOTES

BASIC ITALIAN
Instructions, Cultural Notes and Conversations

Le Regioni: (The regions)

Some of the regions specialty foods will be mentioned in the next paragraphs The reader will keep in mind that it is not the purpose of this book to expand on the subject of cooking, but including part of it can be of cultural value.

Piemonte:

This region yields the Barolo wine, well known worldwide. Also the Barbaresco as well as Dolcetto are very much used everywhere. Piedmont 's capital, Turin, is noted for the Grissini (breadsticks). Fontina cheese originates from these parts. Risotto, pasta, bollito misto (boiled meats) are very popular. Asti Spumante, Vermouth are used to accompany desserts or torrone, (nougat candy).

Questa regione produce il famoso vino 'Barolo', conosciuto dappertutto. Anche il 'Barbaresco e il Dolcetto' vengono usati in molti posti. La capitale del Piemonte, Torino, e' nota per i Grissini. Il formaggio 'Fontina' origina da queste parti. Inoltre il risotto, pasta, bollito misto sono molto popolari. Lo Spumante Asti e il Vermouth vengono serviti con i dolci or torrone.

Veneto:

Here seafood reigns, with its razor-shell clams called 'cannolicchi' and granseole (Adriatic crabs) accompanied by risotto nero (black rice, blackened with cuttle-fish ink). The Venitians are also very fond of risi e bisi (rice and peas) or fegato alla veneziana (liver venitian style). The chocolate dessert called 'Tirami Su' has originated in this region. The prevailing wine from Veneto is Valpolicella, but the vineyards proliferate in Merlot and Cabernet.

Qui il pesce predomina, con le volgole locali, chiamate 'cannolicchi' e i granchi, chiamati, 'granseole' vengono serviti col risotto nero. Ai Veneziani piacciono molto, anche, i risi e bisi o fegato alla veneziana. Il famoso dolce 'Tirami Su' origina in questa zona. Il vino piu' conosciuto del Veneto e' 'Valpolicella', ma ci sono molti altri Merlot e Cabernet.

Toscana:

In Florence's region the bread baked in wood-fired ovens is very good and much used. Il pane toscano, sliced, toasted with garlic, olive oil (extra virgin) form the bruschetta (a tasty appetizer), fresh tomatoes and fresh basil can be added. The Florentines favor white kidney beans with their bistecca alla fiorentina (steak). In the land of the Chianti, Brunello di Montalcino and Vino Nobile di Montepulciano, red wines, are common. Preferred sweets are the almond cookies from Prato, called 'Biscotti di Prato' and Siena's panforte (a sweet fruit cake) served with sweet vin santo.

NOTES

In Firenze c'e' il pane, che viene cucinato nei grandi forni di mattoni, ed e' ottimo. Col pane toscano si fa la bruschetta, che e' fatta a fette, tostate con aglio, olio, pomodori freshi e basilico. Un piatto favorito dai Fiorentini e' la bistecca alla fiorentina con fagioli bianchi. Nella terra del Chianti, ci sono anche Brunello di Montalcino e Vino Nobile di Montepulciano, che sono vini rossi. I dolci preferiti sono i biscotti di Prato e il panforte di Siena che vengono serviti con vin santo.

Umbria:

Some of the finest olive oil and black truffles are produced in this region. Dried pasta is also made here. Lamb, poultry and rabbit are popular, as well as cured meats such as 'prosciutto' widely known. The local wine is the white Orvieto along with the reds Torgiano and Sagrantino di Montefalco.

Alcuni dei piu' buoni olio d'oliva e tartufi neri vengono fatti in questa regione. Pasta asciutta si fa anche qui. Agnello, pollo e coniglio sono molto popolari, come anche il prosciutto e simili prodotti. Il vino locale e' Orvieto e anche i vini rossi Torgiano e Sagrantino di Montefalco.

Lazio:

Rome and surroundings abound in many tasty foods. Among the most popular are the antipasto with tomatoes topped with mozzarella, olive oil and fresh basil (a delicious appetizer), spaghetti alla carbonara, (with eggs, cheese and bacon), and bucatini alla matriciana (with tomatoes, salt pork and the pungent cheese, called Pecorino Romano). The local soil lends itself to growing very tasty vegetables, such as peas and artichokes and others. Pizza Romana is also popular with the wine of choice Frascati and Marino.

Molti cibi saporiti si trovano in Roma e dintorni. Fra questi ci sono l'antipasto, fatto con pomodori e mozzarella e olio e basilico fresco, spaghetti alla carbonara, e bucatini alla matriciana. Il suolo e' molto fertile e adatto a crescere vegetali di sapore come piselli, carciofi e altri. La pizza romana e' molto popolare e viene servita col vino 'Frascati e Marino.'

Campania:

Due to the volcanic soil and its fertility, the production of vegetables and fruits in Naples and surrounding areas is not only abundant but it has a unique flavor, difficult to duplicate elsewhere. Seafood is plentiful in the gulf of Naples. Buffalos graze near Salerno and Capua, from which the world reknown Mozzarella di Bufalo and Provola are obtained. Neapolitans are very fond of street food, meaning potato crockets, fried vegetables, rice balls, and small fried pizzas, plain or stuffed with a variety of stuffings. These foods are easily available almost every where in the city. The most popular pizza is the Margherita, a basic pizza with tomatoes, mozzarella, oil and basil. The city yields also sweet pastries, gelati and sweet espresso. Greco, Fiano, Taurasi are the wines.

NOTES

La produzione dei vegetali e frutta a Napoli e dintorni, non solo e' abbondante ma ha un sapore unico. Cio' e' dovuto al suolo vulcanico e fertile, ed e' difficile duplicare altrove. C'e' anche un'abbondanza di pesce nel Golfo di Napoli. Vicino Salerno e Capua si trovano i bufali da cui si ottengono la famosa mozzarella e la provola. Ai Napoletani piace molto cibo fritto, come i crocche' di patate, vari vegetali fritti, palle di riso e pizze fritte con vari ripieni. Questo tipo di cibo si trova dappertutto in centro della citta'. La pizza piu' famosa e' la 'Margherita' che e' una pizza sottile, larga con pomodori freschi, mozzarella, olio e basilico, cucinata al forno. Molto popolari sono anche una grande varieta' di dolci, meglio conosciuti come paste, gelati, e caffe' espresso. Greco, Fiano, Taurasi sono i nomi di alcuni vini locali.

Sicilia:

The first pasta industry originates in this region, founded by Arabs, using grain from fields planted earlier by the Romans. Again, because of the fertile volcanic soil, the vegetable and fruits grown here are very tasty. Herbs, spices, capers are used in abundance in the local recipees. Pasta con le sarde (with sardines) is very popular. Ricotta is used in pasta fillings and pastries. A famous pastry is Cannoli, using ricotta as the main ingredient; the Cassata (a chocolate-coated sponge cake) is among the top of an array of delicious desserts. The marsala and sweet Moscato Passito di Pantelleria and Malvasia delle Lipari are well known sweet wines.

La prima industria di pasta origina in questa regione e fu fondata dagli Arabi, che usavano il grano che era stato pianteggiato, molto tempo prima, dai Romani. Anche qui, come in Campania, il suolo e' vulcanico e fertile, ed e' per questo che i vegetali e frutta cresciuti in queste parti sono molto saporiti. Le spezie, i vari odori come basilico, prezzemolo eccetera, e capperi vengono usati molto nelle ricette locali. Pasta con le sarde e' un piatto molto comune. La ricotta si usa nei ripieni di pasta e dolci. Un dolce locale e' 'Cannolo' dove si usa la ricotta come l'ingrediente principale; la Cassata e' anche molto conosciuta in questa zona. Il Marsala e Moscato Passito dolce di Pantelleria e Malvasia delle Lipari sono vini dolci molto popolari.

Sardinia:

This island rocky's coast has available a variety of fish, including rock lobsters, mullets and others. Among the most popular dishes are 'su farru' (mint and barley soup), 'malloreddus' (semolino gnocchi with meat or tomato sauce) and 'favata' (fava beans stewed with pork). Each village specializes in its own style of bread, although the flatbread 'pane carasau' and its variation called 'carta da musica' (music paper) is liked by all. The sweet wine Malvasia and the strong liquor Mirti are predominant.

NOTES

La costa rocciosa di quest'isola genera una varieta' di pesci, tra cui le aragoste. Tra i piatti piu' popolari si trovano 'su farru', che e' una minestra, e 'malloreddus', che sono gnocchi di semolino con salsa di pomodori, e 'favata', che sono le fave con carne di maiale. Ogni villaggio si specializza in un particolare tipo di pane, sebbene il pane piatto 'pane carasau' e una sua variazione chiamata 'carta da musica' vengono goduti da tutti. Il vino dolce 'Malvasia' e il liquore forte 'Mirti' sono predominanti.

Vocabulary:

Fagioli	Beans	Olio	Oil	Pentola	Pan
Piselli	Peas	Aceto	Vinegar	Cucinare	To cook
Pomodori	Tomatoes	Prezzemolo	Parsley	Basilico	Basil
Pane	Bread	Forno	Oven	Ordinare	To order
Acqua	Water	Bicchiere	Glass	Conto	Bill

Practice reading aloud the following conversation:

Mario e Teresa vanno a fare spese al mercato locale:
(Mario and Teresa go shopping at a local open produce market)

Topic: To buy fresh produce for a nice meal:

Teresa: Buon giorno, se avete i peperoni, desidero un chilo.
(Good morning, if you have peppers, I would like a kilo)

Venditore: I peperoni sono gialli, verdi e rossi, quali vuole?
(Vendor) (the peppers are yellow, green and red, which ones would you like?)

Teresa: Uno verde e il resto misti, per piacere.
(One green and the rest mixed, please)

Venditore: Va bene Signora, che altro?
(OK, lady, what else?)

Teresa: Desidero cucinare la peperonata, ho bisogno di melenzane, vero?
(I would like to cook the 'peperonata', I need eggplants, right?)

Venditore: Si, certo, per fare la peperonata ci vogliono peperoni e melenzane.
(Yes, sure, to make the peperonata, you need peppers and eggplants.)

NOTES

BASIC ITALIAN
Instructions, Cultural Notes and Conversations

Teresa: Va bene, mi dia mezzo chilo di melenzane e del prezzemolo.
(OK, give me half e kilo of eggplants and some parsley.)

Mario: Teresa ma non prendi anche la frutta?
(Teresa, aren't you getting any fruit?)

Teresa: Si, certo, che frutta preferisci?
(Yes, sure, what kind do you like?)

Mario: Mi piacciono le ciliege, ma decidi tu, compri quello che vuoi.
(I like cherries, but you decide, buy what you want.)

Teresa: Quanto costa un chilo di ciliege? E le pesche quanto al chilo?
(How much does a kilo of cherries cost? and the peaches?)

Venditore: Le ciliegie costano due mila al chilo, e le pesche tre mila.
(The cherries cost two thousand lire per kilo, the peaches three.)

Teresa: Va bene, mi dia mezzo chilo di ciliege e un chilo di pesche.
(OK, give me half a kilo of cherries and one kilo of peaches)

Vemditore: Va bene, che altro?
(OK, what else?)

Teresa: Un'insalata e una radicchio, desidero fare un'insalata mista.
(A green lettuce and a radicchio lettuce, I wish to make mixed salad)

Venditore: Il conto ora?
(The bill now?)

Teresa: Si, per piacere.
(Yes, please)

Venditore: Ecco il conto, Signora.
(Here is the bill, lady)

Teresa: Ecco dieci mila lire.
(Here is ten thousand)

Venditore: Ecco il resto, arrivederci e grazie.
(Here the change, goodbye and thank you)

Teresa: Arrivederci
(Goodbye)

NOTES

Mario: Bene, che altro ti serve?
(Well, what else do you need)

Teresa: Devo comprare la carne ancora, ma prima ci prendiamo un caffe'?
(I must buy the meat yet, but, first let's get a cup of coffee)

Mario: Si, certo, desidero qualche cosa col caffe', forse un dolce.
(Yes, sure, I like something with the coffee, maybe a pastry)

Teresa: Si, anch'io desidero un dolce e dopo torniamo a casa.
(Yes, I would like a pastry too, and afterward we will go home)

Mario: Va bene, Teresa, oggi sono a tua disposizione, ma hai detto di comprare la carne.
(OK, Teresa, today I am at your disposal, but you said you had to buy the meat.)

Teresa: Si, hai ragione dopo aver comprato la carne andiamo a casa.
(Yes, you are right, after we buy the meat, we go home)

Mario: Va bene.

NOTES

BASIC ITALIAN
Instructions, Cultural Notes and Conversations

CAPITOLO TREDICI (13)

I tempi dei verbi.

In chapter three and four the verbs were introduced and the present tense was conjugated for regular, auxiliary and some irregular verbs. In this chapter there is a list of the various tenses, most of which, will be covered in this book and the conjugation of the future tense of the verb 'parlare'. It is good practice to learn the conjugation gradually and proceed only if previous tense is reasonaly understood and memorized.

There are simple tenses and compound tenses. Compound tenses usually require an auxiliary or other verb.

SIMPLE TENSES
(TEMPI SEMPLICI)

COMPOUND TENSES
(TEMPI COMPOSTI)

Present Indicative:	I speak (io parlo)	Present Perfect:	I have spoken (Io ho parlato)
Imperfect Indicative:	I was speaking (io parlavo)	Past Perfect:	I had spoken (Io avevo parlato)
Past Absolute:	I spoke (io parlai)	Past Anterior:	I had spoken (Io ebbi parlato)
Future Indicative:	I will speak (io parlero')	Future Perfect:	I will have spoken (Io avro' parlato)
Pres. Subjunctive:	You speak (tu parli)	Past Subjunctive:	You have spoken (tu abbia parlato)
Imperfect Subj.:	If I spoke (se io parlassi)	Past Perf. Subj.:	If I had spoken (se io avessi parlato)
Pres. Conditional:	I would talk (io parlerei)	Past Conditional:	I would have talked (io avrei parlato)
Imperative:	You speak (parla)		
Pres. Infinitive:	To speak (parlare)	Past Infinitive:	To have spoken (aver parlato)
Past Participle:	Spoken (parlato)		
Present Gerund:	Speaking (parlando)	Past Gerund:	Having spoken (avendo parlato)

NOTES

Basically all the tenses listed above complete the list of tenses available, some of the tenses may be referred differently in different books, however the function of each tense remains the same.

Not all the above tenses will be covered in this book, mostly because some are not used as much and other are used in rare circumstances. Also to maintain the simplicity, objective of this book, only the most common tenses will be explained. Each tense will be covered in its entirety and the tenses to be covered will be introduced gradually.

Parlare = To speak   Futuro = Future Tense

Io   parl**ero'**   (I will talk)   noi   parl**eremo**

tu   parl**erai**   voi   parl**erete**

lui, lei   parl**era'**   loro   parl**eranno**

As previously mentioned, the stem of the verb is present in all conjugation, please, note in the above conjugation of the future tense of verb "Parlare" half the word in each person is the stem of the verb and the rest is the ending (shown above in bold).

To form the future of any regular verb ending in are, the ending is added to the stem of the verb.

For example the endings for the future tense are: **ero'   - erai - era'**
eremo - erete - eranno (as shown above)

If we apply these endings to another 'are' verb, such as "Cantare" (to sing), we have:

cant**ero'**   -   cant**erai**   cant**era'**

cant**eremo**   cant**erete**   cant**eranno**

Practice reading the following sentences, focusing on the verbs:

Domani io parlero' al dottore.   (Tomorrow I will speak to the doctor)

Tu parlerai in italiano.   (You will speak in Italian)

Maria, questa volta, parlera' in inglese.   (Maria, this time, will speak in English)

Lei parlera' al gruppo.   (She will speak to the group)

NOTES

Noi parleremo alla conferenza.	(We will speak at the conference)
Voi parlerete agli studenti.	(You will speak to the students)
Essi parleranno alla maestra.	(They will speak to the teacher)
I signori parleranno ai clienti.	(The gentlemen will speak to the clients)
Loro parleranno in dialetto.	(They will speak in dialect)
Esse parleranno nella lingua madre.	(They, fem. will speak in the mother language)

Vocabulary:

parlare	(to speak)	lingua	(language)
chiamare	(to call)	telefono	(telephone)
visitare	(to visit)	amico	(friend)
imparare	(to learn)	italiano	(italian)
abitare	(to live)	citta'	(city)
studiare	(to study)	lezione	(lesson)
desiderare	(to wish)	dolce	(sweet)
lavorare	(to work)	ufficio	(office)
mangiare	(to eat)	mela	(apple)
ascoltare	(to listen)	radio	(radio)
guardare	(to watch)	televisione	(television)
bruciare	(to burn)	fuoco	(fire)

NOTES

BASIC ITALIAN
Instructions, Cultural Notes and Conversations

Esercizio 15:

Inserire il verbo giusto nelle frasi seguenti:

1. Mia sorella _____ (will speak) a tuo fratello.

2. Mio fratello _____ (will speak) al maestro.

3. Mario e Giacomo _____ (will speak) al professore.

4. Tu _____ (will speak) al dottore.

5. Noi _____ (will speak) al giardiniere.

Read the following paragraph, focusing on the verbs:

E' l'alba. La mattina si **avvicina** e il giorno **comincera'** fra breve. Maria si **sveglia** e **sente** gli uccelli che **cantano** in giardino. La finestra **aperta fa entrare** in camera aria fresca che **piace** a Maria. Lei **pensa** all'amica che **arrivera'** in poco tempo per **progettare** il loro viaggio in Italia. **Progetteranno** di **andare** a **visitare** le citta' piu' famose in Italia. **Saranno** in Roma per tre giorni e poi **prenderanno** il treno per Sorrento, dove **affitteranno** una macchina e **faranno** un giro della costa Amalfitana.

It is dawn. The morning is approaching and the day will soon begin. Maria wakes up and hears the birds singing in the garden. The open window lets fresh air in the room, which Maria likes. She thinks of her friend, who will soon arrive to plan their trip to Italy. They will plan to go to visit some of the most famous cities in Italy. They will be in Rome for three days, and then they will take the train to Sorrento, where they will rent a car and will take a tour of the Amalfitan coast.

NOTES

BASIC ITALIAN
Instructions, Cultural Notes and Conversations

CAPITOLO QUATTORDICI (14)

Il futuro dei verbi ausiliari.

Verbs - Future Tense of auxiliary verbs 'essere and avere' plus the Imperfect Indicative of 'essere' and the Past Absolute of the verb 'Avere' All three of these tenses are among the 'simple tenses'.

Essere = To be　　　　　　　Future Tense

Io	saro'	(I will be)	noi	saremo	(we will be)
tu	sarai	(you will be)	voi	sarete	(you, pl, will be)
lui, lei	sara'	(he or she will be)	loro	saranno	(they will be)

Avere = To have　　　　　　　Future Tense

io	avro'	(I will have)	noi	avremo	(we will have)
tu	avrai	(you will have)	voi	avrete	(you, pl, will have)
lui, lei	avra'	(he or she will have)	loro	avranno	(they will have)

---

1. The 'Imperfect Indicative' tense expresses repetitive or continuous action in the past. The 'Past Absolute' tense expresses action completed in the past: ex: Mentre mangiavo, il telefono squillo' (While I was eating, the phone rang).

2. It is difficult to compare the Italian conjugation with the English conjugation. The structure of the Italian grammar, including the verbs, is very different from the English equivalent. Therefore the student should learn the application of the usage of the Italian verbs.

NOTES

Essere = To Be					
		Imperfetto = Imperfect Indicative			
Io	ero	(I was)	noi	eravamo	(we were)
tu	eri	(you were)	voi	eravate	(you, pl, were)
lui, lei	era	(he or she was)	loro	erano	(they were)

Avere = To Have					
		Passato Remoto = Past Absolute			
Io	ebbi	(I had)	noi	avemmo	(we had)
tu	avesti	(you had)	voi	aveste	(you, pl, had)
lui, lei	ebbe	(he or she had)	loro	ebbero	(they had)

Practice reading the following sentences:

Domani saro' a casa tua.	(Tomorrow I will be at your house)
Tu avrai un cane.	(You will have a dog)
Che sara', sara'	(What will be, will be)
In Aprile saremo in Italia	(In April we will be in Italy)
In cucina avremo una mela	(In the kitchen we will have an apple)
Ragazzi, domani sarete a scuola	(Boys, tomorrow, you will be in school)
Gli studenti saranno in classe	(The students will be in class)
I signori avranno un ombrello	(The gentlemen will have an umbrella)

NOTES

Mentre parlavo al telefono, il campanello suono' (While I was on the phone, the bell rang)

Parlavi sempre sottovoce (You were talking, always, with a low voice)

Parlavamo con loro con piacere (We were talking with them with pleasure)

Parlammo con loro ieri (We talked with them yesterday)

Noi parlavamo in inglese (We were talking in english)

Noi parlammo in italiano (We talked in Italian)

Tu parlasti con Mario (You spoke with Mario)

Tu parlavi con Mario quando il campanello suono' (You were talking with Mario when the bell rang)

Il presidente parlo' alla gente alla televisione (The president spoke to the people on TV)

Gli studenti parlarono in italiano (The students spoke in Italian)

Gli studenti parlavano bene (The students were talking well)

Le signore parlavano continuamente (The ladies were talking continuously)

Vocabulary:

entrata	(entrance)	porta	(door)
uscita	(exit)	portone	(main door)
proibito	(forbidden)	portiere	(attendant)
ascensore	(elevator)	posta	(mail)
palazzo	(building)	ufficio postale	(post office)
scale	(stairs)	terzo piano	(third floor)
biglietto	(ticket)	telefonino	(intercom)
finito	(finished)	pacco	(package)

NOTES

sedile   (seat)   numero   (number)

compartimento   (compartment)   lettera   (letter)

Exercise 16:

Tradurre le frasi seguenti:

1. You will be on the train in compartment D, seat number 10 for Florence.

2. We will have a letter from Maria.

3. Maria will have a package from Italy.

4. Giovanni was talking continuously.

5. Maria talked well in class.

6. We will be in Rome in April.

7. Maria spoke well of the trip

8. While Giovanni was speaking, the phone rang.

9. The boys will be at my house tomorrow.

10. The students spoke Italian in class.

NOTES

BASIC ITALIAN
Instructions, Cultural Notes and Conversations

CAPITOLO QUINDICI (15)

Riepilogo (Review).

In this chapter a synopsis of the grammar covered so far will be presented. The objective is to learn the construction of a basic sentence and gradually adding other components to it, to make the sentence longer and even compound. Once the student learns how to build a sentence, he or she can write any sentence using different vocabulary. The same is true with the verbs and their various tenses.

The basic sentence consists of: subject, verb, object., with transitive verbs. Ex: Luigi mangia una mela. (Luigi eats an apple), Lui mangia una mela (He eats an apple), Lei mangia una mela. (She eats an apple). With intransitive verbs the sentence consists of **subject, verb**. Ex: Luigi cammina (Luigi walks), Luigi parla (Luigi speaks).

In Italian when using a noun, a definite or indefinite article is required. Ex. Il ragazzo mangia una mela.

In order to write a correct sentence, in Italian, the gender of nouns must be determined so that the articles can be matched to the nouns, both in gender and in number.

Most words ending in 'o' are masculine singular, changing the ending to 'i' for the plural.

Most words ending in 'a' are feminine singular, changing the ending to 'e' for the plural.

Definite Articles: **il** (m) - **la** (f) for singular.
    i (m) - **le** (f) for plural

Indefinite Articles   **un or uno** (m) - **una** (f)

After determining the gender and number of the **subject**, everything else in the sentence has to agree **with it**.   Examples:
  Il gatto e' nero (The cat is black) - La ragazza e' Italiana (The girl is Italian)

  I gatti sono neri   (The cats are black) - Le ragazze sono Italiane   (The girls are Italian)

  Un ragazzo mangia il gelato   (A boy eats ice cream)

  Una ragazza mangia il gelato   (A girl eats ice cream)

  Uno studente mangia il gelato   (A student eats ice cream)

Note: Uno is used in front of words beginning with s + consonant. (see Chapter 2)

NOTES

Verbs:

Most verbs end in **'are' - 'ere' - 'ire' for the infinitive, and there are regular and irregular verbs.**

To determine the stem of a verb simply delete the ending. Ex. parlare (to speak) - The stem is **'parl'** the stem is present in all the forms of the conjugation; by adding the appropriate ending to the stem a particular tense is formed.

Examples: La maestra parla lentamente (The teacher talks slowly)

   prendere (to take)   - the stem is '**prend**'

   noi prendiamo il caffe" (we have coffee) - Maria prende la borsa (Maria takes the purse)

   sentire (to hear)   -   the stem is **'sent'** -

   noi sentiamo un rumore (We hear a noise) - Maria sente un rumore (Maria hears a noise)

Irregular verbs have a rather unique conjugation and to learn them is to memorize them. The endings of irregular verbs are, sometimes, similar to the endings of regular verbs. The helping verbs have, also, a slightly different conjugation that regular verbs and also need to be studied and memorized. The verb 'essere' has the first person singular and the last person plural (Io sono e loro sono) (I am, they are) written and pronounced exactly the same, however the context of the sentence will definitely indicate the meaning.

Agreement of adjectives:

All adjectives have to agree in gender and number with the noun which they modify. First determine the gender and number of the noun and then the adjectives matches the ending of the noun. Ex.: Che lungo giorno (What a long day), giorno is the noun and lungo is the adjective, as the student can see the endings of both words are the same. Sometimes the confusion occurs when using adjectives ending in 'e' such as 'grande' or 'gentile'. The rule is that all words, including adjectives, excluding few exceptions, which end in 'e' in the singular, normally end in 'i' for plural, **regardless of gender.**

Examples: Il ragazzo e' gentile   - La ragazza e' gentile   (The boy or the girl is kind)

   I ragazzi sono gentili - Le ragazze sono gentili (The boys - the girls are kind)

The word 'Nipote', which is a noun and means nephew or niece. How is the gender determined? It depends on the sentence. If a sentence reads or states: 'Ho due nipoti' it is impossible to determine, unless further specified or the logical question would follow such a statement as whether they are boys or girls.

NOTES

If a sentence reads or states: 'Il mio nipote e' molto alto' then it is clear, by the rest of the sentence, that the gender is masculine.

The adjectives bello and buono are modified when used in front of masculine singular nouns:

Examples: Un buon pranzo   (A good dinner)   -   Buon giorno (Good morning)

Un bel pranzo   (A nice dinner)   -   Un bel giorno (A nice day)

The verb 'Stare' (To stay, to be) is often used in greeting other people. The present tense is as follows: Sto, Stai, Sta, Stiamo, State, Stanno.

The pronoun 'Lei' is used when addressing a person directly. When using this pronoun the third person of any verb is required. 'Lei' is referred to as a polite 'you' versus 'tu' which is the familiar 'you'.

Examples: Lei come sta oggi, Signor Rossi? (How are you, today, Mr. Rossi?) (Polite form)

Tu come stai, Mario?   (How are you, Mario?)   (Familiar form)

It is, also, worth repeating that the pronouns are not necessary in a sentence when the right verb is used.

Example: Come sta oggi, Signor Rossi or Come stai, Mario?

Both formats above are correct.
Prepositions and prepositions combined with the definite article:

The simple prepositions are: di (of or from) - da (from or by) - a (at or to) - su (on) in (in) - con (with) - per (per) and tra or fra (among).
The prepositions combined with the definite article are: del (of the) - dal (from the) - al (to the) - col (with the) and sul (on the). The prepositions with the definite article listed here are only in the masculin singular form, for the complete presentation see chapter nine.

Examples: Sto a casa di Mario (I am at Mario's house) Arrivo da Venezia (I arrive from Venezia)
Il colore del vestito (The color of the dress) Gli spaghetti al dente (spaghetti not overcooked)
Past Participle: Ex. Ho **mangiato**, sono **andato** (I have eaten or I ate, I have gone or I went)

The past participle is used, primarily, with the auxiliary verbs, 'essere, avere'
This tense is formed by removing the ending are/ere/ire of any verb in the infinitive form and replacing it with **ato/uto/ito.**

NOTES

Examples:

Ho parlato (I have spoken) - Hai mangiato? (Have you eaten?) - Sono stato (I have been)-

At this point it is helpful to repeat that there are Transitive and Intransitive verbs.
Transitive verbs are those which **require** a direct object to complete the meaning.
Intransitive verbs are verbs which **do not require** a direct object to complete the meaning.
Examples of transitive verbs are: Mangiare (To eat), Vendere (To sell), Sentire (To hear) etc.
Examples of intrasitive verbs are: Arrivare (To arrive), Andare (To go), Partire (To leave) etc.

Usually transitive verbs require the verb 'avere' (to have) as a helping verb.
Usually intransitive verbs require the verb 'essere' (to be) as a helping verb.

Examples:
Ho mangiato una mela (I have eaten an apple) - Ho venduto una casa (I have sold a house) -

Ho sentito un rumore (I have heard a noise)   -

Sono arrivato in Seattle (I have arrived in Seattle) Sono andato a Milano (I have gone to Milan)

Sono partito da Seattle   (I have left from Seattle) -

Possessive Adjectives:

The possessive adjectives are: mio (my), tuo (your), suo (his), nostro (our), vostro (your), loro (their). These adjectives, listed above, are in the masculin and singular form. The possessive adjectives, like other adjectives need to agree with the noun they modify in gender and number. For the complete list see chapter five.
Possessive adjectives, when used in front of nouns, often require the definite article, except when referring to members of the immediate family.

Examples: Il mio vestito (my dress) - Il tuo libro (your book) - Il nostro tavolo (our table)

Mio padre (my father) - Tuo fratello (my brother) - Suo zio (his uncle)

In the feminine singular: Mia madre (my mother) - mia sorella (my sister) - Sua zia (her aunt).

Comparisons of Adjectives:

There is a positive, comparative and superlative for each adjective.

NOTES

Bravo, piu' bravo, bravissimo - buono, piu' buono, buonissimo - bello, piu' bello, bellissimo-

These adjectives are shown in the three formats. Let's see how they are used:

Examples: Michele e' proprio bravo (Michael is really good or able) (referring to skill level)

        Mario e' piu' bravo di Michele (Mario is better than Michele)

        Mario e' bravissimo (Mario is best)

        Mario e' il piu' bravo (Mario is **the** best)

Verb Tense - Future:

The future tense of a regular are/ere/ire verb is formed by replacing the ending with 'ero' or 'iro' for example: Mangero' (I will eat), Parlero' (I will speak), Sentiro' (I will hear).

The future tense of the auxiliary verbs are irregular and follow: Saro' (I will be), sarai (you will be), sara' (he or she will be), saremo (we will be), sarete (you, pl, will be), saranno (they will be).
Avro' (I will have), avrai (you will have), avra' (he or she will have), avremo (we will have), avrete (you, pl, will have), avranno (they will have).
Examples: Mangero' a casa mia stasera (I will eat at my house tonight) - Parlero' alla classe domani (I will speak to the class tomorrow) - Sentiro' il telefono da qui (I will hear the phone from here).
Saro' a casa tua alle sette (I will be at your house at seven)-Che sara', sara' (What will be, will be.)
Saremo in Seattle Sabato (We will be in Seattle Saturday) - Saranno a Milano in Dicembre
                                            (They will be in Milan in December).

The original basic sentence used at the beginning of this chapter is 'Luigi mangia una mela', let's expand on this sentence:

    Luigi mangia una buona mela   (Luigi eats a good apple)

    Luigi ha mangiato una buona mela   (Luigi ate a good apple)

    Luigi mangera' una buona mela   (Luigi will eat a good apple)

Luigi mangia una buona mela e Maria mangia una pera
(Luigi eats a good apple and Maria eats a pear)

    La mela di Luigi e' piu' buona della pera di Maria (Luigi's apple is better than Maria's
                                            pear).

NOTES

CAPITOLO SEDICI (16)

La leggenda di S. Gennaro a Napoli
e lo Scoppio del Carro a Firenze

San Gennaro is the patron of Naples and was the bishop of Benevento in 305 A.D. The legend of San Gennaro has been passed down from generation to generation for many centuries. He was a martyr and he was persecuted among the early Christians. He was condemned to death by a proconsul named Timoteo, who happen to die mysteriously a few days after his order of killing San Gennaro by decapitation, was carried out.

The legend is about a follower of San Gennaro, who collected the martyr's blood, right after his death and kept it in a phial which was united with San Gennaro's relics. Allegedly San Gennaro condemnation to death took place in 'Solfatara', near Naples and was buried in Campo Marciano, near Solfatara. Years later the relics of San Gennaro were transferred to Naples. At present time there is a church in Solfatara, named after the Saint and another larger one downtown Naples and it is in this one church that the miracle of S. Gennaro occurs at least twice a year.

The legend refers to the liquefying of the blood, kept in the phial, of San Gennaro on his day, the 19th of September each year. It is at this celebration that thousands of people gather in the large church in Naples and wait for this happening to occur. It has been said that if the blood does not liquefy, people in Naples, are fearful something bad is likely to happen in that year. It seems that this miracles occurs several times a year, but it is more likely to be expected to happen on the 19 of September each year.

Occasionally, this event occurs at different times besides on the dates expected. In 1978 when Cardinal Cooke of New York visited this San Gennaro church in Naples, the blood liquefied, much to the delight of the Cardinal as well as the people present at the time, as they saw it as a way that San Gennaro was trying to manifest himself to them or communicate with his followers. It is a very meaningful happening to the Neapolitans and a very moving happening to witness for anyone, providing being in the crowd of people is no problem.

In Italy most people are named after Saints' names, therefore Italians celebrate 'nameday' as well as birthdays. Equally important is the celebration to the Italian people. Men in Italy, whose name is Gennaro (Jerry), celebrate their nameday on the 19 of September, the day of San Gennaro.

NOTES

BASIC ITALIAN
Instructions, Cultural Notes and Conversations

Traduzione:

San Gennaro e' il patrono di Napoli ed era il Vescovo di Benevento nell'anno 305 A.D. La leggenda di San Gennaro e' passata da generazione a generazione per molti secoli. Egli era un martire e fu perseguitato con gli altri Cristiani. Egli fu condannato a morte, decapitato, da un proconsole, che si chiamava Timoteo, il quale mori' misteriosamente pochi giorni dopo che la condanna, contro San Gennaro, fu eseguita.

La leggenda e' circa un devoto di San Gennaro, il quale raccoglio' il sangue del Santo, subito dopo la morte del martire e lo mise in una fiala, che fu tenuta insieme alle altre relinquie. San Gennaro fu condannato a morte e la condanna venne eseguita in un posto chiamato 'Solfatara', vicino Napoli e fu seppellito in 'Campo Marciano', vicino alla Solfatara. Anni dopo le relinquie di San Gennaro furono transportate a Napoli. Ora esiste una chiesa in Solfatara, che si chiama 'la chiesa di San Gennaro' in suo onore e un'altra chiesa e' a Napoli. In quest'ultima chiesa il miracolo avviene minimo due volte all'anno.

La laggenda si riferisce al sangue, nella fiala, che si scioglie nel giorno di San Gennaro, il 19 Settembre ogni anno. E' a questa celebrazione che migliaia di gente viene a vedere. Si dice che se il sangue non si scioglie quell'anno, qualcosa di brutto succede alla citta'. Si dice che questo miracolo occorre molte volte all'anno, ma e' piu' comune che occorre il giorno della Festa di San Gennaro, il 19 Settembre ogni anno.

Ogni tanto quest'evento succede durante altri giorni, diversi dai precedenti. Nel 1978 quando il Cardinale Cooke di New York visito' la chiesa di San Gennaro a Napoli, il sangue si sciolse, alla gioia dei devoti e coloro che erano presenti. Cio' sembrava che San Gennaro volesse manifestarsi ai suoi devoti. Vedere questo miracolo e' un'esperienza molto commovente e piena di significato per i Napoletani, e per ognuno, per cui stare nelle folle non e' un problema.

In Italia, la maggioranza delle persone vengono chiamate come i nomi dei Santi; quindi si celebra l'onomastico, come anche il compleanno. Tutte e due le celebrazioni sono importanti agli Italiani.
Gli uomini, in Italia, il cui nome e' Gennaro, celebrano l'onomastico il 19 Settembre, il giorno della Festa di San Gennaro.

Lo Scoppio del Carro (the Explosion of the Cart)

This tradition takes place in Florence on Easter Sunday in the main church, Duomo, every year. Its origin dates back to the year circa 1000 A.D. and it was started by a family called 'Pazzi' residents of Florence. It seems that a member of this family, in 1535 participated to the crusade, as a leader of the Florentines troops, to conquer Jerusalem. He fought so valiantly that he was given the permission to use his coat of arms and was given some precious stones, which were brought back to Florence. These stones were used to spark a

NOTES

'holy fire' for religious ceremonies. The fire symbolized the resurrection of Jesus, defined as "light of the world'.

These stones were moved from church to church. As each church was destroyed over the years, the stones were moved till they were stored, permanently in Chiesa di SS. Apostoli, where they are still there today. Two of these stones are used to start the 'holy fire' in the Cathedral in Florence each Easter. Over the years, when the last member of this family died the local City Hall continued the tradition.

This tradition, on Easter Sunday, consists of placing a large cart, loaded with fireworks, painted and decorated with flowers, pulled by two white oxen, in front of the main doors of the Cathedral in Florence.
The cart is escorted by a group of flag throwers, dressed in costumes from the 15th century, who, upon arriving in the square in front of the Cathedral, perform an exhibition of the flag throwing. Between the main altar and the cart outside there is a wire connecting the two. After the procession starts, with the Bishop, and as soon as he is seated at the altar, a small rocket, in the shape of a dove, is lit and released, on the wire from the altar to the cart to begin the fireworks. The fireworks last about an half an hour and as soon as they start, all the other churches in Florence ring their church bells. Then Mass begins. At the end of the Mass a good will message is given to the people present in many different languages with last being in English and given by the Bishop.

It is a very impressive event to attend and quite a pleasant attraction both for the Florentines and for the tourists. Again, as in Naples, thousands of people attend this tradition.

Traduzione

Questa tradizione avviene a Firenze il giorno di Pasqua nella Cattedrale ogni anno. L'origine va intorno all'anno Mille A.D. e fu iniziata da una famiglia, chiamata 'Pazzi', residenti di Firenze. Pare che un membro di questa famiglia, nel 1535 partecipo' ad una crociata, come condottiero di truppe Fiorentine, alla concquista di Gerusalemme. Egli combatto' cosi valorosamente che gli fu dato il permesso di usare il suo stemma e delle pietre prelevate. Queste pietre vengono usate per accendere 'il fuoco sacro' per le cerimonie religiose. 'Il fuoco sacro' rappresenta la resurrezione di Gesu', definito la 'luce del mondo'.

Queste pietre sono state mosse da chiesa a chiesa. Ogni volta che una chiesa veniva distrutta, le pietre venivano rilocate finche' vennero poste permanentemente nella Chiesa di SS. Apostoli, dove sono tenute tutt'ora. Due di queste pietre vengono usate per cominciare il 'fuoco sacro' nella cattedrale a Firenze ogni Pasqua. Quando l'ultimo membro della famiglia 'Pazzi' mori', il Comune continuo' la tradizione.

Questa tradizione, a Pasqua, consiste di un carro con fuochi d'artificio, dipinto e decorato con fiori, portato da due buoi bianchi, e posto di fronte alla Cattedrale. Questo carro viene scortato dalle guardie del Comune, indossando costumi del cinquecento. Le guardie, arrivati

NOTES

a destinazione, fanno un'esibizione con le bandiere. Tra l'altare maggiore e il carro, fuori la chiesa, viene messo un filo metallico che congiunge i due. Quando la processione nella Cattedrale finisce e il Vescovo si siede, un fuoco, nella forma di una colomba, viene acceso e viene mandato sul filo metallico sino a raggiungere il carro fuori, dove accende i fuochi d'artificio.

I fuochi durano quasi mezz'ora e come cominciano, le altre chiese suonano le campane. La Messa comincia. Alla fine della Messa un messaggio di auguri viene dato alle persone presenti, in diverse lingue con l'ultimo dato in Inglese e dal Vescovo.

Questo e' un evento molto interessante a vedere e piacevole, sia per i Fiorentini che per i turisti. Di nuovo, come a Napoli, migliaia di persone vengono a vedere questa tradizione.

Practice reading the Italian version of above text, studying each paragraph, more than once.

NOTES

BASIC ITALIAN
Instructions, Cultural Notes and Conversations

CAPITOLO DICIASETTE (17)

I verbi riflessivi

The reflexive verbs are used in the Italian language very frequently. Often the reflexive verbs in Italian do not correspond to reflexive verbs in English. Therefore, it is very difficult and strongly discouraged from translating a sentence literally.

The structure of the Italian grammar is very different than the English counterpart. It is easier for a student of the language to focus on the context of a sentence written in Italian, rather than translating **literally**. Plenty examples of the reflexive verbs and their application will follow. Sometimes verbs, which are reflexive in Italian, are not in English.

There are basically three kinds of reflexive verbs:

Intransitive reflexive verbs:	(accorgersi, annoiarsi)	(to take notice, to be annoyed)
Reciprocal reflexive verbs:	(noi ci amiamo)	(we love each other)
Transitive apparent reflexive verbs:	(mi compro un libro)	(I buy myself a book)

Some verbs can function both as regular verbs and as reflexive. However the reflexives are always preceded by pronouns mi, ti, si, ci, vi, si. The infinitive is also formed slightly differently,

examples: Lavare (to wash), Lavo i piatti (I wash the dishes) - regular transitive verb.

Lavarsi (to wash oneself), Mi lavo (I wash myself) - reflexive verb

Fermare (to stop), Fermo il pullman (I stop the bus) - regular transitive verb

Fermarsi (to stop oneself), Mi fermo (I stop myself) -reflexive verb

---

Divertirsi = To enjoy oneself

Io	mi	diverto	Noi	ci	divertiamo
Tu	ti	diverti	Voi	vi	divertite
Lui, Lei	si	diverte	Loro	si	divertono

NOTES

BASIC ITALIAN
Instructions, Cultural Notes and Conversations

Chiamarsi =	**To call oneself**				
io	mi	chiamo	noi	ci	chiamiamo
tu	ti	chiami	voi	vi	chiamate
lui, lei	si	chiama	loro	si	chiamano

Alzarsi =	**To get oneself up**				
io	mi	alzo	noi	ci	alziamo
tu	ti	alzi	voi	vi	alzate
lui, lei	si	alza	loro	si	alzano

Lavarsi =	**To wash oneself**				
io	mi	lavo	noi	ci	laviamo
tu	ti	lavi	voi	vi	lavate
lui, lei	si	lava	loro	si	lavano

Il sole cominciava a filtrare tra le tende nella camera di Teresa. All'improvviso il telefono suono' e Teresa risponde: 'ciao, Caterina, come stai? Mi alzo fra pochi minuti, mi faccio la doccia e mi vesto e poi ti vengo a prendere'. Le due amiche avevano progettato di andare ad una gita insieme. Alla gita ci sono molti altri amici, e spesso si divertono molto a parlare o nuotare o giocare a palla a volo con i loro amici. Teresa arriva a casa di Caterina in ritardo e dice a lei: 'mi dispiace che sono in ritardo, ma andiamo e vedrai che ci divertiamo.'

The sun began to show through the curtains in Teresa's bedroom. Suddenly the phone rang and Teresa answered: 'hi, Caterina, how are you? I will get up in a few minutes, I'll take a shower and get dressed and then I'll come to pick you up. The two friends had planned to go to an outing together. At the site of the outing or picnic there will be many

NOTES

other friends of the girls. Often they enjoy themselves at these gatherings, they enjoy talking with their friends, or swimming or playing volley ball. Teresa arrives late at Caterina's house and says to her: 'I am sorry I am late, but let's go and you'll see, we will enjoy ourselves.'

In some cases, the pronoun instead of preceding the verb, it can be attached to it instead. For example:
tu ti vesti or vestiti (you dress yourself), tu ti diverti or divertiti (enjoy yourself). Either form is correct. Its use depends on the context of the sentence. The attached form is probably used more in colloquialism.

Examples of application of reflexive verbs:

Quando vai al cinema, divertiti.	(When you go to the movies, enjoy yourself)
A che ora ti alzi al mattino?	(What time do you get up in the morning)
Come si chiama tua sorella?	(What your sister's name?)
Prima di mangiare ci laviamo le mani	(Before dinner we wash our hands)
Come ti senti, Maria?	(How are you feeling, Maria?)
Gli uomini si siedono al bar.	(The men sit themselves at the bar)
Le donne si vestono in nero.	(The women dress themselves in black)
I bambini si chiamano Gino e Luigi.	(The children's names are Gino and Luigi)
Ella si veste in fretta.	(She dresses herself in a hurry)
La signora a fianco si alza presto.	(The lady next door gets up early)

Esercizio 17:

Underline all the reflexive verbs found in the paragraph above, written in Italian.

NOTES

Esercizio 18:

Match the sentences from column one with those in column two.

1. Per arrivare in Italia
2. La Signora domanda
3. Mi chiamo Caterina e
4. Le ragazze si alzano alle sette e
5. Quando andate al cinema
6. I ragazzi vanno in centro e
7. Quando siamo con i nostri amici
8. Prima di mangiare i ragazzi
9. Mi lavo sempre le mani
10. Teresa si alza molto presto

a. ci vogliono molte ore di volo.
b. tu come ti chiami?
c. come si chiama questa bella bambina?
d. si divertono.
e. si lavano le mani.
f. voi a che ora vi alzate?.
g. per andare al lavoro.
h. dove vi sedete?
i. quando torno in casa dal giardino.
k. ci divertiamo molto.

NOTES

CAPITOLO DICIOTTO (18)

Altri verbi riflessivi

There are many other forms and uses of the reflexive verbs, also the various tenses are used depending on the context of the sentence. Reflexive verbs are much more used in the Italian language than in English. Again one cannot translate literally as, often, a reflexive verb or an idiom does not have an equivalent meaning, in English, or other languages.

1. The word '**piacere**' is used to mean different meanings, as follows:

    Piacere or favore   (favor), ex: Mi fai un piacere?   (Will you do me a favor?)

    Per piacere or per favore   (please)

    Piacere di conoscerla or piacere   (pleased to meet you)

    Piacere   (to please)

The verb 'Piacere' does exist as a regular verb, however it is used mostly in the reflexive form, and more importantly, it is used in the third person singular or third person plural the majority of times. This form can be best explained with examples:

Mi piace il gelato	(I like ice cream or ice cream is pleasing to me)
Ti piace la cioccolata	(You like chocolate or chocolate is pleasing to you)
Gli piace la pizza	(He likes pizza or pizza is pleasing to him)
Le piace quel negozio	(She likes that store or that store is pleasing to her)
Ci piace questo film	(We like this movie or this movie is pleasing to us)
Vi piace questo vino	(Do you (pl) like this wine or this wine is pleasing to you)
Piace a loro questa casa?	(Do they like this house or this house is pleasing to them)

Notice that all the examples above include the verb in the third person singular in the present tense and the adjectives and nouns used are all in the singular.

NOTES

Rule: When the noun is in the singular, the verb needs to be in the third person singular, **regardless** of the reflexive pronouns preceding the verb.
When the noun is in the plural, the verb needs to be in the third person plural, **regardless** of the reflexive pronouns preceding the verb.

Examples:

Mi piacciono i fiori rossi   (I like red flowers or red flowers are pleasing to me)

Ti piacciono le ciliege?   (Do you like cherries or are cherries pleasing to you?)

Gli piacciono i maccheroni? (Does he like maccheroni or are maccheroni pleasing to him)

Le piacciono le pizze.   (She likes pizze (pl) or pizze are pleasing to her)

Ci piacciono i gelati.   (We like ice cream or ice cream is pleasing to us)

Vi piacciono queste case? (Do you like these houses or are these houses pleasing to you?)

Questi fiori piacciono a loro. (These flowers are pleasing to them or they like these flowers)

2. Another verb used mostly in the third person singular is: **'dispiace'**, but it is preceded by the reflexive pronouns, examples:

    Mi   dispiace   (I am sorry)

    Ti   dispiace   (Do you mind or it is not pleasing to you)

    Gli   dispiace che il cugino e' malato.   (He is sorry that the cousin is sick)

    Le   dispiace che tua madre e' malata.   (She is sorry that your mother is sick)

    Ci   dispiace non poter venire a casa vostra. (We are sorry we cannot come to your house)

    Vi   dispiace se guido?   (Do you mind if I drive?)

Dispiace tanto a loro che la cugina e' malata. (They are very sorry the cousin is sick)

As shown in above examples the subject of a sentence is determined or indicated by the correct use of the reflexive pronouns.

NOTES

3. **'Mi e' successo'** (it has happened to me). The phrase **'e'successo'** can be preceded by any of the reflexive pronouns (mi, ti, gli, le, ci, vi, loro) depending on the subject of the intended sentence.

4. A list of some commonly used reflexive verbs, in the infinitive tense, follows:

    a. arrangiarsi (to make do or improvise)   d. trovarsi   (to find oneself)
    b. comportarsi (to behave oneself)   e. chiamarsi   (to call oneself)
    c. sentirsi   (to feel referring to health) f. accomodarsi (to make oneself confortable)

Study the following conversation and find the reflexive verb forms.

Una conversazione fra due amici

Luigi: Ciao Mario, come stai? e' molto tempo che non ti vedo.
(Hi Mario, how are you, it is a long time since I saw you)

Mario: Ciao Luigi, si, e' vero che non ci vediamo da molto tempo.
(Hi Luigi, yes, is true, we haven't seen each other for a long time.)

Luigi: Che fai di nuovo?
(What you are doing these days)

Mario: Non abito piu' con i miei genitori, ho trovato un appartamento con due altri amici.
(I don't live with my parents anymore, I have moved in an apartment with two friends)

Luigi: Veramente? Come ti trovi?
(Really, how is it working?)

Mario: Mi trovo molto bene, la padrona di casa, che si chiama Teresa, ci porta un pranzo ogni tanto.
(It is working very well, the landlady, whose name is Teresa, brings us dinner every now & then)

Luigi: Che brava padrona di casa, e' gentile, ma le altre volte chi cucina?
(What a nice landlady, she is kind, but who cooks the other times)

Mario: Facciamo a turno, ma ci arrangiamo.
(We take turns, but we make do or manage)

NOTES

Luigi: Continui ad andare all'Universita' e come studi con tanta gente in casa?
(Are you continuing College? and how can you study with so many people at home)

Mario: Si, vado all'Universita'. I miei amici si comportano abbastanza bene, anche loro vanno all'Universita' e quando uno di noi studia o si prepara per un esame, gli altri capiscono.
(Yes, I go to College. My friends behave themselves very well, they also go to College and when one of us has to study or prepare for an exam, the others understand.)

Luigi: E' una buona situazione. Mi fa piacere.
(It is a nice situation. I am pleased)

Mario: E tu che fai?
(And you, what are you doing?)

Luigi: Io ho finito la laurea in Economia e Commercio ed ora lavoro per una Compagnia nel Dipartimento 'Marketing'
(I have finished the degree and graduated in Business Administration and now I work for a Company, in the Marketing Department.)

Mario: Ti piace questo lavoro?
(Do you like this job?)

Luigi: Si, certo. Ogni tanto devo viaggiare e cio' mi fa piacere.
(Yes, sure. Every now and then I must travel and this I like.)

Mario: Cerchiamo di vederci un poco piu' spesso e fare qualcosa insieme.
(Let's try to see eachother a little more often and do something together)

Luigi: Si, e' una buona idea, ti do il mio numero di telefono di casa e di lavoro e possiamo metterci d'accordo una sera di uscire.)
(Yes, it is a good idea, I give you my phone number, for the house and for work and we can agree on an evening to go out together.)

Mario: Benissimo. Ti telefonero'. Ecco il mio numero e puoi chiamarmi anche tu. Ciao, piacere di averti rivisto.
(Great. I will call you. Here is my number and you can call me too. Bye, pleased to have seen again.)

NOTES

Exercise 19:

Inserire il verbo corretto nelle frasi seguenti:

1. Buongiorno, Maria, _____ oggi?
   _{how are you}

2. Ciao, Anna, oggi _____ e tu?
   _{I do not feel well}

3. Mi dispiace, _____ mal di testa?
   _{do you have}

4. Si, ho mal di testa, ma _____ d'altro.
   _{let's speak}

5. Si, va bene. _____ nella 'Mall' andiamo a prendere un cappuccino?
   _{we find each other}

6. Va bene, _____, andiamo.
   _{I like that}

7. Le due ragazze _____ contente e _____ a stare insieme.
   _{Appear} _{they enjoy themselves}

8. Oggi _____ al cinema.
   _{one goes}

9. Il giovane _____ Mario.
   _{calls himself}

10. Siamo andati al cinema e _____.
    _{enjoyed ourselves}

NOTES

BASIC ITALIAN
Instructions, Cultural Notes and Conversations

CAPITOLO DICIANNOVE (19)

Altri tempi semplici dei verbi, Il condizionale e il gerundio.

Parlare - To speak		**Condizionale**			
io	parlerei	(I would talk)	noi	parleremmo	(we would talk)
tu	parleresti	(you would talk)	voi	parlereste	(you, pl, would talk)
lui, lei	parlerebbe	(He, she would talk)	loro	parlerebbero	(they would talk)

Il Gerundio:

This tense is formed by simply removing the last three letters from the infinitive form of the verb and adding 'ando' in its place. ex. **Parl (are) - Parlando.** This is true for the 'are' verbs only. With verbs ending ere/ire, the new ending is 'endo' ex. **Vend (ere) - Vendendo - Sent (ire) - Sentendo.**

Following is a list of verbs in the infinitive tense with their respective gerund tenses:

Parlare	-	Parlando	(Speaking)	Cucinare	-	Cucinando	(Cooking)
Mangiare	-	Mangiando	(Eating)	Partire	-	Partendo	(Leaving)
Vendere	-	Vendendo	(Selling)	Vedere	-	Vedendo	(Seeing)

Usually this tense, depending on the context of the sentence, is used by itself or with the auxiliary verb 'Stare' as shown in the following table:

---

io	sto	parlando	(I am talking)	noi	stiamo parlando	(we are talking)
tu	stai	parlando	(you are talking)	voi	state parlando	(you are talking)
lui, lei	sta	parlando	(He, she is talking)	loro	stanno parlando	(they are talking)

NOTES

The verb 'stare' can be used in different tenses with the gerund remaining the same, ex:

io	stavo	parlando	(I was talking)	noi	stavamo	parlando
tu	stavi	parlando		voi	stavate	parlando
lui, lei	stava	parlando		loro	stavano	parlando

or

io	staro'	parlando	(I will be talking)	noi	staremo	parlando
tu	starai	parlando		voi	starete	parlando
lui, lei	stara'	parlando		loro	staranno	parlando

L'Imperativo:

This tense is used in giving a command to another person. It does not have a first person as usually commands are given to others. Ex: Mangia, bambino (eat, child), mi scusi (excuse me), si accomodi (make yourself confortable).
The most frequently used forms of this tense are the second and third persons. The second person is used when one is familiar with person talking to, such as a friend, relative, child. The third person is used when using the polite 'Lei', examples:

Mi scusi, Signore, che ore sono?   (Excuse me, Sir, what time is it?)

Signora, si accomodi nel salotto.   (Mam, make yourself confortable in the living room)

Per piacere, si segga.   (Please seat yourself) (pol.)

Scusa, Mario, ti do fastidio?   (Excuse me, Mario, am I bothering you?)

Studia, ragazzo, devi imparare.   (Study, boy, you must learn)

When using the imperative, with verbs ending in 'are' the second person ends in 'a' and the third person ends in 'i' as in 'scusa, scusi' or 'mangia, mangi'.
With verbs ending in ere/ire the opposite is true. The second person ends in 'i' and the third person ends in 'a' as in 'siedi, segga' or 'senti, senta'. There is no first person in the imperative tense.

NOTES

Il Congiuntivo:

The present and the imperfect subjunctive are tenses used less frequently, however a brief mention of their usage follows. This tense is used to express an action, which is desiderable or possible; the following sentences will demonstrate its applications:

Spero che vada tutto bene durante il viaggio.   (I hope it all goes well during the trip)

Prego che sia tutto pronto.   (I pray that everything is ready)

Speriamo che la maestra non perda la pazienza.   (Let's hope that the teacher does not lose patience)

Se fossi ricco, comprerei una bella macchina.   (If I were rich, I would buy a nice car)

Se Maria fosse stata attenta, avrebbe capito.
(If Maria had been attentive, she would have understood)

Marco, **camminando e parlando** con il suo amico, non si accorse che Caterina lo passo' e lo saluto' brevemente. Caterina era una ragazza molto attraente e andava alla stessa scuola di Marco. Infatti Marco ha tentato molte volte di parlare con Caterina e invitarla fuori. Se Marco avesse la possibilita' di vedere Caterina, **parlerebbe** di molte cose. Lui dice all'amico: '**scusa**, devo parlare con Caterina' e corre via.

Mark, walking and talking with his friend, does not realize that Caterina just passed and said hello to him, briefly. Caterina was a very attractive girl and went to the same school as Mark. Infact Mark tried many times to talk with her and to ask her out. If Mark had the possibility to see Caterina, he would talk about many things with her. He says to his friend: 'excuse me, I must speak with Caterina' and he runs off.

Read above paragraphs and analyze the structure of the sentences in Italian. Study the tenses and compare them with the presentation of the tenses in this chapter.

Vocabulary:

Ecco or qui	(here)	Allora	(now then)	Perche'	(because)
Ebbene	(well then)	Nulla	(nothing)	Nessuno	(nobody)
Quindi	(now then)	Ma	(but)	Percio'	(therefore)

NOTES

Niente   (nothing)   Mai   (never)   Non c'e' di che   (don't mention it)

Neanche   (neither)

Esercizio 20:

Match the sentences from column one with those in column two:

1. Se fossi ricco.   a. la donna vede molti fiori.

2. Spero che la maestra.   b. farei un bel giro del mondo.

3. Camminando in giardino.   c. comprerei una bella macchina.

4. Mario stava parlando al telefono.   d. si accomodi in salotto.

5. Caterina parlerebbe con l'amica ma.   e. non perda la pazienza.

6. Io parlerei con mia sorella molto spesso. f. quando il campanello suono'

7. Mi scusi, dove si trova.   g. la stazione centrale del treno.

8. Senta, Signora, questa e'.   h. se abitasse piu' vicino.

9. Entri, prego, Signore, e.   i. proprio una buona marca.

10. Se vincessi la lotteria.   l. deve andare a fare spese.

NOTES

BASIC ITALIAN
Instructions, Cultural Notes and Conversations

CAPITOLO VENTI (20)

I pronomi

Si parla di una gita alla spiaggia. Le due amiche decidono di andare alla spiaggia **con** altre **loro** amiche. Caterina dice all'amica: 'io posso venire **con te** e poi andiamo a prendere le altre, va bene?' risponde l'amica: 'si, va bene, ma **mi fai** un piacere e telefoni e **le** inviti a venire **con noi**?'

They are talking about an outing to the beach. The two girlfriends decide to go to the beach with their other girlfriends. Caterina says to her friend: 'I can come with you and then we can go get the others, ok?' Her friend answers: 'yes, ok, but do me a favor and call and invite them to come with us.

The object pronouns are an important part of a sentence. In Italian the object pronouns are several and are used according to the function, the context the sentence indicates. In many cases it is very difficult to translate literally, therefore it is suggested to study the examples, more than the rules.

Object Pronouns	
(Precede the verb)	(Follow the verb) - (Used with prepositions con, per, a, etc.)
mi	me
ti	te
si	se (stesso, stessa)
ci	noi
vi	voi
si	loro

Note: Pronouns preceding the verb are used only in the reflexive, ex. si lava le mani (he washes his hands).
Also do not confuse them with the other meaning of these words: si =(yes), se =(if).
Notice that noi, voi, loro are the same as subject pronouns.

NOTES

Examples:

Mi piace il tuo vestito	(I like your dress)
Ti piacciono le pesche?	(do you like peaches?)
In questa casa si mangia alle sei	(in this house we eat at six)
Ci vediamo domani	(we'll see each other tomorrow)
Vi incontro domani in centro	(I will meet you tomorrow downtown)
I ragazzi si chiamano Mario e Luigi	(the boys names are Mario and Luigi)

Maria, vieni con me al cinema?	(Maria, come with me to the movies?)
Il fratello va con te, sei d'accordo?	(the brother goes with you, do you agree?)
Egli sta bene da se stesso.	(he is fine by himself)
Ragazzi, venite con noi.	(boys, come with us)
Posso venire con voi?	(can I come with you?)
Luigi va a pranzo con loro.	(Luigi goes to have dinner with them)

In addition to above pronouns, there are others as follows:

	Masculine	Feminine	Transl.
Third person	lui	lei	(him, her)
" "	lo	la	(him, her, it)
" "	li	le	(them)
" "	gli	le	(to him, to her)

As mentioned previously, the pronouns 'lui' and 'lei' can be used as either subject or object pronouns. The pronouns 'egli' and 'ella' are grammatically the correct form of subject pronouns, however, the pronouns 'lui' and 'lei' have become common use, as subject or object pronouns, in the informal usage of the language.

NOTES

The pronouns 'lo, la, li, le, gli' are generally used before the verb.

Examples:

1. Lui viene a casa mia domani   (He comes to my house tomorrow)

2. Desidero andare con lui.   (I wish to go with him)

3. Lei sa usare il computer.   (She knows how to use the computer)

4. Preferisco andare con lei.   (I prefer to go with her)

5. Bisogna chiamare il cameriere, lo. (It is necessary to call the waiter, I'll do it) chiamo io

6. C'e' una Banca di fronte, la vedi?   (There is a Bank across the street, do you see it)

7. Ci sono due uomini nel negozio, (There are two men in the store, do you see them) li vedi?

8. Ci sono due ragazze in macchina,(There are two girls in the car, do you see them) le vedi?

9. Se vedo Mario, gli dico che sei arrivato. (If I see Mario, I tell him that you arrived)

10. Al compleanno del fratello, gli telefona. (At the brother's birthday, he phones him)

Notes: 'Lei' is also used when addressing a person in a formal way, regardless of gender. (see chapter seven).

Do not confuse the pronoun 'gli' (to him) with the definite ariticle 'gli' (the), the context of the sentence will indicate the meaning.

The object pronouns 'lo, la, li, le' can be attached to the end of verb, as well as preceeding it. Generally the infinitive is used with attached pronoun. Examples of its application will follow.

It is very common in the Italian language to speak formally among people who do not know each other and in other situations as explained in chapter seven. This usage applies also to the object pronouns, therefore some samples of their application follow:

NOTES

LA = You (formal, sing. object pronoun) (used when addressing a person, regardless of gender)

LI, LE = You (formal, plural, masc., fem. object pronoun)

Examples:

1. Lei fa una domanda, io **la** rispondo.   (You ask a question, I will answer)

2. Lei mi canta una canzone, **la** prego.   (You sing me a song, I beg you or please.)

3. Lei compra I biglietti, **la** pago domani.   (You buy the tickets, I will pay you tomorrow)

4. Vedi i Signori? Si, **li** vedo.   (Do you see the Gentlemen? Yes, I see them)

5. Fai entrare le Signore! Si, **le** faccio entrare. (Let the Ladies enter. Yes, I will let them in)

Vocabulary:

persona	(person)	faccia	(face)	piede	(foot)
mano	(hand)	corpo	(body)	orecchio	(ear)
dito	(finger)	occhi	(eyes)	gamba	(leg)

Esercizio 21: Highlight all the pronouns found in the following paragraphs.

> Caterina e Mario andavano a fare spese per comprare un regalo per il compleanno della loro amica. Camminando in centro incontrarono il cugino di Mario e lo invitarono a venire con loro. Il cugino, che si chiama Marco, ando', con piacere, con loro a fare spese. Caterina trova una bella sciarpa e una borsa e non puo' decidere che cosa comprare. Marco dice a Caterina: 'se tu non compri la sciarpa, la compro io 'Va bene, comprala, ed io compro la borsa' rispose Caterina. Quella sera andarono tutti e tre alla festa del compleanno dell'amica, e si divertirono.

Esercizio 22: Tradurre le seguenti frasi:

1. Lui mangia al ristorante ogni giorno con lei.

2. Se tu non compri la sciarpa, la compro io.

3. Ho spiegato che gli telefonero' a mezzogiorno.

4. Mario ha molti amici, li invita a casa.

5. La Signora ha un cane, lo vedi?

6. Gli diamo una mano.

NOTES

BASIC ITALIAN
Instructions, Cultural Notes and Conversations

CAPITOLO VENTUNO (21)

Altri tempi di verbi e la loro funzione

There are simple tenses and compound tenses. Simply the simple tense of a verb does not require an auxiliary, but the compound tense requires the auxiliary verb in Italian.

Esempio: Io parlo or io parlero' -   is a **simple tense.**
          (I speak or I will speak)

          Io ho parlato or io avro' parlato -   is a **compound tense** because it is using
          (I have spoken or I will have spoken)   the auxiliary.

Following is a conversation using the application of above tenses:

Maria: **Io parlo** con Giovanni oggi circa la tua partenza. Lui lavora in una agenzia di viaggi.

Marco: Si, va bene, sai le date della mia partenza? Dopo **io parlero'** con Giovanni.

Maria: Si, le so, amenonche' non le cambi.

Marco: No, non le cambiero'.

Maria: (La settimana dopo la prima conversazione con Marco)
         Marco, senti, **ho parlato** con Giovanni e questo e' l'itinerario, lo spedisco a casa tua. Quando noi parleremo di nuovo, **tu avrai** parlato con Giovanni circa l'itinerario.

Marco: Spero anche che Giovanni trova un buon prezzo.

Maria: Di questo parlerai direttamente con lui.

Marco: Si, va bene, grazie e ciao.

Maria: Prego, ciao.

In Italian the imperfect (parlavo) and the past tense (parlai) are used differently than in the English version. Furthermore often the present perfect (ho parlato) is used much more frequently that the past tense.

NOTES

Following examples will show their applications.

> Esempio: **Io parlavo** con Mario, quando il campanello **suono'**
> (I was speaking with Mario, when the bell rang)

> Esempio: Il mese scorso **parlai** col Direttore della Banca circa un prestito.
> (Last month I spoke with the Director of the Bank regarding a loan)

Parlavo indicates continuous, repetitive past action, while suono' indicates past action. In the second sample, parlai indicates past, remote action.

> Esempio: Ieri **ho cucinato** un buon pranzo per Maria perche' era il suo compleanno.
> (Yesterday I cooked a good dinner for Maria because it was her birthday.)

Ho cucinato indicates more recent past action.

To summarize:

Imperfect (parlavo)	=	continuous, repetitive past action
Past tense (parlai)	=	remote past action
Pres. Perfect (Ho cucinato)	=	recent past action

Following is a conversation using the application of above tenses.

Marco: Mentre parlavo con Caterina ho scoperto che giovedi' e' il compleanno di Maria ed ho cucinato un bel pranzo per lei.

Angela: Che bell'idea, che cosa hai cucinato?

Marco: Ho cucinato per primo, le fettuccine con salsa fresca, poi pollo con spinaci e patatine fritte come contorni, e insalata mista.

Angela: Che buono, e per dolce?

Marco: Faro' il tiramisu' per dolce.

Angela: Bravissimo, sai che io parlai con Maria il mese scorso e lei mi disse che il tiramisu' e' il suo dolce preferito.

Marco: Lo so, e percio' che l'ho fatto.

NOTES

Angela: Sei veramente un genio, Maria sara' molto contenta, devo andare, ci sentiamo, ciao.

Marco: Va bene, ci sentiamo, ciao.

The conditional and the gerund tenses can be used both in simple or compound tenses:
Parlerei (I would talk) is the simple conditional tense.
Avrei parlato (I would have talked) is the compound tense.

Parlando (speaking) is the simple gerund tense.
Sto parlando (I am speaking) is the compound tense.

Following is a conversation using the application of above tenses:

Maria: C'e' un gruppo di stranieri che si raduna in Seattle e si parlano diverse lingue.

Marco: Interessante, posso venire? Io parlerei Italiano.

Maria: Si, certo, ne avrei parlato prima ma non lo sapevo.

Marco : Va bene, quando sara'?

Maria: Non lo so, ma stando in Seattle domani cerchero' di informarmi.

Marco: Parlando di stranieri, spero che ci saranno persone che parlano anche francese, perche' sto prendendo lezioni di francese ed ho bisogno di pratica.

Maria: Va bene, a domani sera, ciao.

Marco: Va bene, grazie, ciao.

Vocabulary:

Suonare	(to play or to ring)	radunare	(to get together)
venire	(to come)	sapere	(to know)
cucinare	(to cook)	Dire	(to say)
prendere	(to take)	cercare	(to seek)

NOTES

BASIC ITALIAN
Instructions, Cultural Notes and Conversations

dopo	(after)	prima	(before)
anche	(also)	amenonche'	(unless)
scorsa	(past)	quando	(when)
diverse	(different)	lingue	(languages)
scoperto	(discovered)	contorno	(side dish)
straniero	(foreign)	mese	(month)

Esercizio 23:

Fill in the blanks in the following sentences:

1. Marco ha scoperto che giovedi' e' il _____ di Maria.

2. Marco _____ il tiramisu' per dolce per Maria.

3. Marco ha preparato gli spinaci e patatine fritte per _____.

4. Per primo, Maria, giovedi' ha mangiato_____.

5. Maria_____ l'insalata mista.

6. Che lingua Marco spera che si parla nel gruppo di stranieri?_____.

7. Il gruppo di stranieri si_____ in Seattle per parlare diverse lingue.

8. Nel gruppo di stranieri si_____ principalmente l'Italiano.

NOTES

BASIC ITALIAN
Instructions, Cultural Notes and Conversations

CAPITOLO VENTIDUE (22)

Gli avverbi e la loro applicazione

Era presto di mattina e **gia'** il sole cominciava a spuntare e dorava le cime degli alberi, che affiancavano, come per proteggere, il fiume. L'acqua scendeva **lentamente** da sopra e copriva la maggior parte delle pietre o rocce nel fiume. In certi punti l'acqua passava molto piu' **rapidamente** che in altri posti. Gli uccelli cinguettavano **dolcemente,** volando tra le cime degli alberi. Guardando il continuo movimento dell'acqua uno sembra di acquistare un senso di calma, serenita', come se ci si distaccasse **lentamente** dalla realta' e quasi sognasse ad occhi aperti. Ecco arriva un pescatore in cerca di un posto ideale per pescare. Il pescatore salta da roccia a roccia molto **attentamente** e **lentamente** e si prepara a pescare.

It was early in the morning and already the sun began to come out and it was gilding the top of the trees, which were on each side of the river, as in a protective fashion. The water came down slowly from the top and it covered most of the rocks in the river. In certain places the water ran much more rapidly than in other places. The birds were chirping and flying among the top of the trees. Looking at the continuous movement of the water, one seems to obtain a feeling of calm, serenity, as tho' one can detach himself, slowly, from the reality and almost daydream. Here comes a fisherman, looking for an ideal spot to fish. He jumps from rock to rock, very cautiously and slowly, and prepares to fish.

As shown in the paragraph above, the Italian version, there are several adverbs used. To point them out, the adverbs have been highlighted in bold. The main characteristic of adverbs is that they do not change and they modify the meaning of other words.

The adverbs can modify the meaning:

1) of a verb: scendeva lentamente

2) of an adjective: cosi bello

3) of another adverb: assai lentamente

There are, principally, three types of adverbs; plenty of examples will be given later on in this chapter to indicate their applications.

NOTES

Avverbi di luogo: (Adverbs of placement)	dove (where), dovunque, (anywhere), qui or qua (here), su (on or up), giu' (down), quassu' (up here), quaggiu' (down here), li' or la' (there), lassu' (up there), laggiu' (down there), sopra (above), sotto (below), accanto (next to), avanti (forward), davanti (in front of), dietro or indietro (behind), vicino (near), lontano (far), oltre (beyond), altrove (elsewhere), dentro (inside), fuori (out).
Avverbi di tempo: (Adverbs of time)	ora (now), ancora (more), allora (then), oggi (today), ieri (yesterday), domani (tomorrow), gia' (already), immediatamente (immediately), prima (before), poi (afterwards), dopo (after), presto (soon), tardi (late), stamani (this morning), stasera (this evening), stanotte (this night), subito (rightnow), spesso (often), sempre (always), mai (never), raramente (rarely), infine (at last), finalmente (finally).
Avverbi di modo: (Adverbs of manner)	cosi (so), si (yes), gentilmente (gently), sinceramente (sincerely), francamente (frankly), lietamente (happily), tristemente (sadly), lentamente (slowly), pigramente (lazily), velocemente (rapidly), fortemente (strongly), altrimenti (otherwise), ugualmente (equally), similmente (similarily), diversamente (differently), invano (useless) adagio (slow), bene (well), male ((ill), piano ((slowly), forte (strong), volentieri (willingly).

Other adverbs include:

Avverbi di quantita':	Molto (much), poco (little), abbastanza (enough), troppo (a lot), alquanto (some), altrettanto (as much), appena (scarcely).
Avverbi di affermazione:	Certo (sure), certamente (certainly), sicuro (sure), davvero (really), sicuramente (surely), indubbiamente (undoubtedly), precisamente (precisely).

Avverbi di interrogazione: perche'? (why), dove? (where), quando? (when), come? (how).

Esempi di avverbi di luogo:

1. I ragazzi cercano un negozio dove comprare un computer.

2. Dovunque si va, si trova da mangiare.

3. Qui non si fuma. Qua si parla Italiano.

NOTES

4. Devi camminare sempre in su per arrivare alla cima.

5. Per parlare con Mario, devi scendere giu'.

6. Vieni quassu' e parliamo.

7. Vieni quaggiu' e ti leggo una storia.

8. Da li' o la' si vedono le montagne.

9. Lassu' c'e' un bel ristorante.

10. Laggiu' c'e' il mare.

11. La signora abita sopra, al terzo piano.

12. La tua amica ti aspettamo sotto il ponte.

13. Mario ti incontra accanto al Museo.

14. La macchina continuo' ad andare avanti.

15. Ci incontriamo davanti all'ufficio postale.

16. C'e' un piccolo negozio dietro al ristorante.

17. La maestra abita vicino alla ragazza.

18. La famiglia abita lontano dalla studentessa.

19. Oltre il fatto che e' tardi, non voglio andare.

20. Quando non trovi qualcosa, cerchi altrove.

21. Bisogna cambiare aria dentro la casa.

22. In primavera si sta spesso fuori.

Esempi di avverbi di tempo:

1. Ora non e' tempo di uscire.

2. Mario voleva ancora spaghetti.

3. Si parla di tante cose, allora, oggi, parliamo di questo soggetto.

NOTES

4. Ieri si rimase in casa, ma domani usciremo.

5. E' gia' mezzogiorno e devo telefonare a Maria immediatamente.

6. Prima o poi si deve fare.

7. Dopo che apri il negozio andai a fare spese.

8. Si fa presto a concludere.

9. Stamani sono arrivata all'ufficio tardi.

10. Stasera c'e' un bel film alla televisione.

11. Stanotte si dormira' bene.

12. Subito puliamo la tavola e come sempre giochiamo a carte.

13. Vado al cinema spesso, ma vado raramente al teatro.

14. Non sono mai stata in Russia.

15. Finalmente abbiamo finito infine.

Esempi di avverbi di modo:

1. Si, il ponte e' cosi alto.

2. Gentilmente la signora le spiego' il processo.

3. L'uomo era sinceramente mortificato.

4. Francamente non posso fare questo lavoro.

5. Si offri' ad andare lietamente.

6. Le signore andarono a visitare l'amica malata tristemente e lentamente.

7. La ragazza leggeva il giornale pigramente di domenica.

8. Mario guidava velocemente.

9. Bisogna tenerlo fortemente, altrimenti non funziona.

10. L'Italiano e il Francese sono ugualmente difficili ad imparare.

11. Dobbiamo fare le cose diversamente.

NOTES

12. E' invano andare a scuola se non si studia.

13. Si cammina adagio per piacere.

14. O bene o male si va avanti.

15. Per piacere parli piano.

16. Questo e' un mobile forte.

17. La donna va all'ufficio volentieri.

Esempi di altri avverbi:

1. Molto poco non e' abbastanza per questo lavoro.

2. Ho mangiato troppo.

3. Metti una tazza d'acqua in questa pentola e altrettanto in quella.

4. Appena l'acqua bolle, aggiungi il sale.

5. Vieni al ricevimento? Si, certo, sicuramemte.

6. Quando torni a casa? Indubbiamente ritorno, precisamente quando, non lo so.

7. Come si dice questa parola in Inglese?

8. Perche' questa strada e' chiusa? e dove si va per andare in citta'?

Vocabulary:

Mettere	(to put)	aggiungere	(to add)	bollire	(to boil)
Chiusa	(closed)	ricevimento	(party)	mobile	(piece of furniture)
tornare	(to return)	ritornare	(to return)	venire	(to come)
tazza	(cup)	pentola	(pot)	cima	(top)
fumare	(to smoke)	mare	(sea)	strada	(street)

NOTES

Esercizio 24:

Match phrases from column I with those from column II:

1.	L'impiegato andava all'ufficio e	a.	Il Museo d'arte?
2.	La mamma aveva cucinato un bel pranzo di	b.	arriva il treno?
3.	Per piacere dove si trova	c.	bisogna camminare velocemente.
4.	Mi scusi, Signore, quando	d.	oggi non e' una bella giornata
5.	Sicuramente gli amici vengono	e.	e lavorava molto.
6.	Per arrivare alla stazione in tempo	f.	la sorella partire per un lungo viaggio.
7.	Ieri era una bella giornata, ma	g.	Belle.
8.	Le due case sono ugualmente	h.	di maccheroni e carne, lietamente.
9.	Tristemente il fratello vedeva	i.	dove fanno e vendono dei buonissimi tipi di pane.
10.	Accanto al ponte c'e' un panificio	j.	a casa mia alle sette.

NOTES

BASIC ITALIAN
Instructions, Cultural Notes and Conversations

CAPITOLO VENTITRE (23)

I tempi composti dei verbi

As mentioned previously in chapter thirteen, there are simple tenses and compound tenses. The simple tenses have one verb, only, or without the auxiliary verb, for examples **io parlo** is a simple tense. The compound tense uses an auxiliary, for example **io ho parlato**; this form uses an auxiliary verb, therefore is defined to be a compound tense. All three conjugations, are, ere and ire have both simple and compound tenses. The auxiliary verbs also have simple and compound tenses.

Ecco un esempio:

> Io parlo spesso con la mia amica al telefono. Oggi ho parlato con lei circa le preparazioni per un ricevimento per celebrare il compleanno del marito. Sara' una sopresa. Sapendo come e' curioso il marito, dobbiamo stare attenti a non dire nulla quando parleremo con lui. Avendo deciso la data, ora bisogna invitare gli altri amici.

> I speak often with my friend on the phone. Today I have spoken with her regarding the preparation for a party to celebrate her husband's birthday. It will be a surprise. Knowing how curious her husband is, we must be careful not to say anything when we will talk with him. Having decided the date, we, now, have to invite other friends.

As you can see in the first line of the paragraph above, written in Italian, has the application of both a simple and a compound tense. In the fourth line you can find a compound tense in 'avendo deciso'.

To summarize a compound tense is formed by using either auxiliary verb (avere, essere) in the various tenses, combined with past participle of any verb. To be more specific examples follow in the various tenses:

Passato prossimo (Present perfect):

> Ho mangiato - Egli ha parlato - Mario e' arrivato.

Trapassato prossimo (Past perfect):

> Avevo mangiato - Lei aveva parlato - Mario era arrivato.

Trapassato remoto (Past anterior): This tense is used rarely.

> Appena che ebbe letto la lettera, comincio' a piangere.

NOTES

BASIC ITALIAN
Instructions, Cultural Notes and Conversations

Futuro anteriore (Future perfect):

    Avro' mangiato - Lei avra' parlato - Mario sara' arrivato.

Congiuntivo passato (Past subjunctive):

    Abbia mangiato - Lui abbia parlato - Mario sia arrivato.

Trapassato (Past perf. subj.):

    Avessi mangiato - Lei avesse parlato - Mario fosse arrivato.

Condizionale passato (Past conditional):

    Avrei mangiato - Lui avrebbe parlato - Mario sarebbe arrivato.

Gerundio passato (Past gerund):

    Avendo mangiato - Avendo parlato - Essendo arrivato.

Note: this last tense is not conjugated, no gender or number is used with it.

Examples:

1. Stamattina ho parlato con Maria.
2. Gino aveva comprato i libri.
3. Per le sei avro' finito di lavorare.
4. Dopo pranzo sono ritornato a casa.
5. Alle otto Mario sara' arrivato.
6. A Marzo saremo arrivati in Italia.
7. Avevo dimenticato le chiavi di casa.
8. Spero che Mario abbia finito.
9. Essendo in piedi per un'ora, ero stanca.
10. Avendo mangiato alle sei, non avevo fame.
11. Spero che Gino sia arrivato a casa.
12. Se tu avessi chiesto aiuto, ti avrei aiutato.
13. Se la ragazza avesse telefonato, sarebbe stato buono.
14. Credo di avere capito.
15. Avendo viaggiato tutto il giorno, era stanco.
16. Essendo stato sul treno molte ore, era intirizzito (stiff).
17. Avrei fatto di tutto per aiutarla.
18. Maria sarebbe venuta a casa mia.
19. La signora aveva detto di pulire la casa.
20. La cameriera aveva pulito la casa.

NOTES

As mentioned earlier in this book the past participle of a regular verb is formed by deleting the ending are or ere or ire and replacing them with ato or uto or ito. Ex. Parlare - Parlato, vendere - venduto, sentire - sentito. This tense is used with either auxiliary verb to form the compound tenses as explained above. However there is no general rule to form the past participle of irregular verbs, so to learn them is to memorize them. Following is a list of some irregular verbs with their respective past participle.

Dire	(to say)	-	detto	fare	(to do)	-	fatto
Leggere	(to read)	-	letto	Spegnere	(to turn off)	-	spento
Mettere	(to put)	-	messo	Accogliere	(to gather)	-	accolto
Ammettere	(to admit)	-	ammesso	Apprendere	(to learn)	-	appreso
Aprire	(to open)	-	aperto	Assumere	(to assume)	-	assunto
Bere	(to drink)	-	bevuto	Chiedere	(to ask)	-	chiesto
Chiudere	(to close)	-	chiuso	Coprire	(to cover)	-	coperto
Cuocere	(to cook)	-	cotto	Decidere	(to decide)	-	deciso
Descrivere	(to describe)	-	descritto	Difendere	(to defend)	-	difeso
Esprimere	(to express)	-	espresso	Essere	(to be)	-	stato
Friggere	(to fry)	-	fritto	Nascere	(to be born)	-	nato
Offendere	(to offend)	-	offeso	Offrire	(to offer)	-	offerto
Prendere	(to take)	-	preso	Promettere	(to promise)	-	promesso
Rimanere	(to remain)	-	rimasto	Rispondere	(to respond)	-	risposto
Scegliere	(to choose)	-	scelto	Scendere	(to go down)	-	sceso
Scoprire	(to discover)	-	scoperto	Scrivere	(to write)	-	scritto
Spendere	(to spend)	-	speso	Succedere	(to occur)	-	successo
Togliere	(to take off)	-	tolto	Tradurre	(to translate)	-	tradotto
Vincere	(to win)	-	vinto	Vedere	(to see)	-	visto

NOTES

BASIC ITALIAN
Instructions, Cultural Notes and Conversations

Vocabulary:

Parola	(word)	Quaderno	(notebook)
Discussione	(discussion)	Argomento	(argument)
Rabbia	(rage)	Colpa	(blame)
Alta voce	(loud)	Sottovoce	(softly)
Disponibile	(available)	Pronto	(ready)
Uscita	(exit)	Entrata	(entrance)
Nuovo	(new)	Vecchio	(old)

Esercizio 25:

Fill in the blanks in the following sentences:

1. Maria _____ all'amica al telefono.
   (has talked)

2. Mario _____ a casa alle otto.
   (has arrived)

3. _____ in citta' molto tempo, conosceva molte persone.
   (having been)

4. Credo che Gino _____ a casa, perche' non stava tanto bene.
   (has remained)

5. Maria _____ bene, se fosse rimasta zitta.
   (had remained)

6. Quando Caterina arrivo', _____ gia'.
   (had eaten)

7. _____ una grande coca cola, Mario non aveva sete.
   (having drunk)

8. Se lei _____ l'occasione, avrebbe parlato molto di piu'.
   (had had)

203

NOTES

9. Non risposi perche' non _____ la domanda.
   (had understood)

10. La donna non poteva entrare in casa perche' _____ le chiavi.
    (had forgotten)

Esercizio 26:

Insert the past participle indicated in the following sentences.

1. Ho _____ un pacco da mia sorella.
   (received)

2. Abbiamo _____ un viaggio bellissimo in Europa.
   (done)

3. Loro non hanno _____ nulla nella lettera.
   (understood)

4. Giovanni non ha _____ al fratello da molto tempo.
   (written)

5. Maria ha _____ molte cose in Italia.
   (bought)

6. Mario ha _____ un libro di Venezia.
   (read)

7. Egli non ha _____ alla mia lettera.
   (answered)

8. Avete _____ la figlia del Direttore?
   (met)

9. I ragazzi hanno _____ molti libri dalla libreria.
   (taken)

10. La nipote ha _____ gli esami all'Universita'.
    (finished)

NOTES

BASIC ITALIAN
Instructions, Cultural Notes and Conversations

CAPITOLO VENTIQUATTRO (24)

I tempi composti per i verbi riflessivi

At this point it is a good idea to review chapter (17), where the simple tenses of the reflexive verbs are explained. This chapter will entail a more in depth view of the reflexive verbs in the compound tenses and their application.

The major point to remember at this time is to be able to form a past participle for regular verbs in all three conjugations (are, ere, ire). Furthermore it is very helpful to study the various tenses of the two auxiliary verbs (avere, essere).

Alzarsi (to get oneself up)

mi alzo (I get myself up)	mi sono alzato (I got myself up)
ti alzi	ti sei alzato
si alza	si e' alzato
ci alziamo	ci siamo alzati
vi alzate	vi siete alzati
si alzano	si sono alzati

In the first column above there is the reflexive simple tense, which happens to be the present tense. In the second column there is the reflexive compound tense of the reflexive verb, shown above.

In the compound tense the auxiliary verb (essere) is used in the present tense. The tense of the auxiliary can be changed to any other tense, with the past participle remaining the same. Examples will show this application. However a rule of agreement must be mentioned first. This rule is **when using the auxiliary verb essere, the past participle agrees, usually, with the subject, in gender and number.** When there are subjects consisting of feminine and masculine gender, the plural masculine will be used.

NOTES

Divertirsi (to enjoy oneself)

mi diverto (I enjoy myself)   mi sono divertito (I have enjoyed myself)

mi divertivo (I was enjoying myself) mi ero divertito (I had enjoyed myself)

mi divertiro' (I will enjoy myself) mi saro' divertito (I will have enjoyed myself)

mi divertirei (I would enjoy myself) mi sarei divertito (I would have enjoyed myself)

Imperativo:

si diverta (third person, formal)   si sara' divertito (you, formal, will have enjoyed yourself)

The reflexive pronouns mi (myself), ti (yourself), si (oneself), ci (ourselves), vi (yourselves), si (themselves), can be used with any of the verbs used above or others, the format remains the same, except in the simple tenses the verb needs to be conjugated for the right person or subject. In the compound tenses the auxiliary verb needs to be conjugated for the right person or subject, and the past participle remains the same. The reflexive pronouns function as object pronouns.

Examples:

Quando vado al cinema, mi diverto molto.
(When I go to the movies, I enjoy myself a lot or I enjoy going to the movies)

Ieri sono andata a vedere un film e mi sono divertito.
(Yesterday I went to see a movie and I have enjoyed myself)

A che ora ti sei alzato stamattina?
(At what time did you get up this morning?)

La bambina si veste da sola. (the little girl dresses herself -by herself-)

Di solito ci alziamo alle otto di mattina, ma stamattina ci siamo alzati alle nove.
(Usually we get up at eight in the morning, but this morning we got up at nine.)

Ieri Maria si e' sentita male, ma oggi si sente bene.
(Yesterday Maria was feeling bad, but today she is feeling well.)

La signora dice all'ospite: "prego, si accomodi nel salotto", l'ospite va nel salotto e si e' accomodato.
(The lady says to the guest: "welcome, make yourself confortable in the living room", the guest went in the living room and made himself confortable.)

NOTES

Vocabulary:

List of some reflexive verbs:

Accorgersi (to perceive)   Arrangiarsi (to make do)   Coricarsi (to put oneself to bed)

Vestirsi (to dress oneself)   Trovarsi (to find oneself)   Ritirarsi (to retire oneself)

Chiamarsi (to call oneself) Divertirsi (to enjoy oneself) Lavarsi (to wash oneself)

Fermarsi (to stop oneself) Riposarsi (to rest oneself) Accomodarsi (to make oneself conft)

Stancarsi (to tire oneself)   Addormentarsi (to fall asleep) Ricordarsi (to remember)

Note that some reflexive verbs or expressions in Italian do not translate into English in the reflexive form.

Esercizio 27:

Inserire i pronomi necessari nelle seguenti frasi:

1. Giovanni, ieri sei andato allo spettacolo, _____ sei divertito?

2. Sono andato presto a dormire e _____ sono riposato bene.

3. La ragazza ____ lava le mani spesso.

4. Le persone in fila _____ sono stancati di aspettare.

5. Gli amici nostri sono andati a sciare e _____ sono divertiti.

6. Non mi ricordo del nostro viaggio, ma dopo avere visto le foto, _____ sono ricordato bene.

7. I ragazzi ____ sono trovati qualcosa da fare.

8. Le ragazze _____ sono trovate qualcosa da fare

9. La mia amica _____ e' divertita molto a leggere la mia lettera.

10. I gentiluomini _____ sono alzati quando entrarono le donne.

11. Prima di mangiare noi _____ siamo lavati le mani.

12. Quando arrivo' la maestra, gli studenti ____ erano seduti gia'.

NOTES

BASIC ITALIAN
Instructions, Cultural Notes and Conversations

CAPITOLO VENTICINQUE (25)

La coniugazione del verbo 'Parlare'

Parlare = To speak

	Pres. Ind.	Imp. Ind.	Past Abs.	Fut. Ind.	Pres. Cond.
io	parlo	parlavo	parlai	parlero'	parlerei
tu	parli	parlavi	parlasti	parlerai	parleresti
lui	parla	parlava	parlo'	parlera'	parlerebbe
noi	parliamo	parlavamo	parlammo	parleremo	parleremmo
voi	parlate	parlavate	parlaste	parlerete	parlereste
essi	parlano	parlavano	parlarono	parleranno	parlerebbero

	Pres. Subj.	Imp. Subj.	Pres. Perf	Past Perf.	Fut. Perf.
io	parli	parlassi	ho parlato	avevo parlato	avro' parlato
tu	parli	parlassi	hai parlato	avevi parlato	avrai parlato
lui	parli	parlasse	ha parlato	aveva parlato	avra' parlato
noi	parliamo	parlassimo	abbiamo parlato	avevamo parlato	avremo parlato
voi	parliate	parlaste	avete parlato	avevate parlato	avrete parlato
essi	parlino	parlassero	hanno parlato	avevano parlato	avranno parlato

NOTES

BASIC ITALIAN
Instructions, Cultural Notes and Conversations

	Past Cond.	Past Subj.	Past Perf. Subj	Imperative
io	avrei parlato	abbia parlato	avessi parlato	--
tu	avresti parlato	abbia parlato	avessi parlato	parla
lui	avrebbe parlato	abbia parlato	avesse parlato	parli
noi	avremmo parlato	abbiamo parlato	avessimo parlato	parliamo
voi	avreste parlato	abbiate parlato	aveste parlato	parlate
essi	avrebbero parlato	abbiano parlato	avessero parlato	parlino

----

Gerund	Past Gerund	Infinitive	Past Participle
parlando	avendo parlato	parlare	parlato/aver parlato

Above is the complete conjugation of the verb 'parlare. It includes some tenses not previously covered. Verbs in the Italian language are complex and difficult to learn, however the more practice one has, the easier one learns. The verb 'parlare' is a regular **are** verb, and the goal of the student is to be able to determine the stem of the verb, which is present throughout the conjugation, and apply the endings to any other regular **are** verb. This chapter can be used also as a reference to the various tenses. Having listed the tenses adjacent to one another, the charts above demostrate the similarities and characteristics of the different tenses.

A word about the usage of some of the tenses:

1. Some tenses are simple tenses in Italian but in the English equivalent take an auxiliary, such as "parlavo (simple tense, imp. ind.) translates in English as I was speaking."

2. The imperfect subjunctive (parlassi) is not used frequently, however when it is, usually, is followed by the conditional tense, example: se parlassi al telefono, parlerei piu' piano (if I spoke on the phone, I would speak slower.)

3. The present perfect (ho parlato) is used more to translate the English past absolute or, more commonly referred to as the past tense, example: ieri ho parlato con Maria (yesterday I spoke with Maria). While the past absolute in Italian is used to indicate more remote past action, example: l'anno scorso parlai con Marco (last year I spoke with Mark.)

NOTES

4. The imperative tense is used to indicate sort of command action, that is why it does not have a first person; example: parla, ragazzo (speak up, boy.) For the third person formal, used when directly addressing a person, it would be scusi or mi scusi (excuse me).

A good rule of thumb for the imperative third person formal is: **Are** verbs end in 'i' (as in scusi) and other **ere or ire** verbs end in 'a' (as in senta=listen).

5. When using the gerund tense the auxiliary verb 'stare' is used, example: sto parlando (I am speaking), or stavo parlando (I was speaking) etc. Again this is true not only with the verb parlare but with all other regular verbs.

Practice reading the following paragraph:

> Si parlava di viaggi all'estero quando Marco arrivo' a casa dell'amico, dove c'era un gruppo di ragazzi. Erano tutti amici, e la maggior parte di questi amici frequentavano la stessa Universita'. Tutti studiavano diversi soggetti, eccetto Marco e il suo amico Davide, che studiavano legge ed erano al terzo anno. Avendo salutato gli amici, Marco comincio' a parlare di un viaggio all'estero. Gia' gli altri amici avevano parlato di organizzare un viaggio insieme per andare all'estero. Parlavano di andare in Central America, cioe' Costa Rica. Marco era molto entusiasta perche' era un suo sogno andare a Costa Rica dopo gli studi. Marco disse: 'proprio oggi ho parlato con un agente di viaggi riguardo il costo e ho scoperto che non costa tanto, ma e' meno costoso andare in primavera invece dell'estate.' Davide disse: 'parlero' con un altro agente di viaggi circa le varie possibilita' di itinerari e prezzi, pero' penso che e' troppo presto per parlare di dettagli, dobbiamo prima finire gli studi.' Gli altri amici acconsentirono e decisero di parlare di nuovo di questo la prossima riunione.

Translation:

> They were talking about a trip abroad when Mark arrived at his friend's house. There was a group of friends, and most of the them went to the same University. They were all taking different subjects, except Mark and his friend David, who were taking Law and they were in the third year. Having greeted his friends, Mark started to talk about a trip abroad. Already the other friends had talked about organizing a trip together abroad. They were talking about going to Central America, specifically Costa Rica. Mark was very enthusiastic because it had been his dream to go to Costa Rica after College. Mark said: 'just today I talked to a travel agent regarding the cost of the trip and I have discovered that it does not cost too much, but it is less expensive to go in the spring rather than in the summer.' David said: 'I will talk to another travel agent regarding the different options of itinineraries and prices, but I think that it is a bit early to talk about details, we must first finish College.' The other friends agreed and decided to talk about it again at the next meeting.

NOTES

Vocabulary:

Arrivare	(to arrive)	frequentare	(to frequent)	scoprire	(to find out)
andare	(to go)	organizzare	(to organize)	salutare	(to greet)
cominciare	(to begin)	acconsentire	(to agree)	decidere	(to decide)
estero	(abroad)	viaggio	(trip)	prima	(first)
insieme	(together)	sogno	(dream)	invece	(instead of)
presto	(soon)	dettaglio	(detail)	di nuovo	(again)

Esercizio 28:

Translate the following sentences into English:

1. Quando arrivo a Firenze l'anno prossimo, come prima cosa, vorrei andare a vedere la Cattedrale al centro.

2. Per fare un viaggio organizzato bisogna fare un itinerario e cercare di seguirlo.

3. Quando una persona va in Italia per turismo, e' molto piu' divertente parlare la lingua Italiana e comunicare nella loro lingua.

4. Avrei parlato piu' piano se avessi saputo che non capivi la lingua.

5. Avendo parlato Italiano spesso con i suoi amici, Marco parlo' l'Italiano molto bene durante il suo viaggio in Italia il mese scorso.

6. Il professore aveva parlato della storia con molti dettagli.

7. Quando Lei mi chiama al telefono, non capisco la lingua molto bene.

8. Spero che parlero' l'Italiano alquanto bene da poter capire gli Italiani quando andro' in Italia l'anno prossimo

9. A Firenze ci sono tanti musei da visitare e anche la Cattedrale, il Battistero e la torre di Giotto e tante altre cose.

10. Ci sono molti bei negozi a Napoli, dove le persone possono fare spese e parlare con i commessi dei negozi.

NOTES

BASIC ITALIAN
Instructions, Cultural Notes and Conversations

CAPITOLO VENTISEI (26)

Un accenno alle tradizioni ed una conversazione

Traditions vary somewhat from region to region. Traditions change a little over the years, but one thing that remains strong in Italy is the family. To the average Italian the family is a very important part of his/her life. It is a way of thinking, which is handed over from generation to generation continuously like any other custom, to respect the family, to stay close to each member, and to care for one another. This mode of behavior is not limited to the nucleus family but to the extended family as well. Older brothers want to protect their younger siblings. All the family members are ready to sacrifice what it takes for the good of the family.

It is not unusual to have older parents live with one of their children as well as children, over eighteen years of age, still living at home and it is not always based on need.

Other customs include the giving of Easter chocolate egg, with the surprise inside, at Easter time. It is given to children Easter day, and to young girls by boyfriends during Easter week, but this latter one may contain a ring as surprise inside the Easter chocolate egg, which is wrapped in fancy, colored cellophane paper. Many stores display these special treats at Easter time in their windows adding to the festivity of the occasion.

Many 'festa' are held throughout the year, for various reasons, some of which include to honor Saints, special occasions. Generally celebrations of a particular event can be quite elaborate depending on the region.

One custom, perhaps exercised in most regions, is called the 'struscio' which is leisure walking, enjoying the surroundings, usually with a friend. This is done in late afternoon and in the most attractive part of town, where stores also are located, or boardwalks along the sea. It seems to be a daily activity that most Italians enjoy doing. However, since most stores close about eight at night, most people will hurry home for the family 'cena' (supper). Almost suddenly the streets are deserted after that time.

At Christmas time there is the famous 'Presepio' which is a miniature scene of Bethlehem with tiny figures of the Holy Family, shepherds and wise men. In Naples most of the churches usually have a version of the 'Presepio', some being more elaborate than others. It is customary to go from church to church to see the various presepi, or as many as possible. On occasions some people may build, a presepio in their house, but this being a complex project, is not a common occurrence.

Many more customs exist and are anjoyed by Italians, but they are too numerous to list here. It would be ideal to be able to attend at least one of these events to see the real thing.

NOTES

BASIC ITALIAN
Instructions, Cultural Notes and Conversations

Una conversazione tra due amici:

Caterina: Ciao Marco, come stai? E' parecchio tempo che non ti vedo.
(Hi Mark, how are you? I haven't seen you in a long time)

Marco: Ciao, bella, che piacere vederti, che fai di bello?
(Hi beautiful, what a pleasure to see you, what are you up to?)

Caterina: Sto progettando un viaggio in Italia con un'amica. Vuoi venire?
(I am planning a trip to Italy with a girlfriend. Do you want to come?)

Marco: Sarebbe bello, ma non posso, devo lavorare, ma parla del viaggio.
(It would be nice, but I can't, I have to work, but talk about the trip.)

Caterina: Andremo verso la meta' di Marzo e torneremo a meta' di Aprile, dopo Pasqua. Mi piace stare per Pasqua in Italia.
(We will go around the middle of March and will come back mid April, after Easter. I like to spend Easter in Italy.)

Marco: Che buona idea. Dove starete il giorno di Pasqua?
(What a good idea. Where will you be on Easter day?)

Caterina: Proprio a Pasqua staremo a Firenze, abbiamo amici che incontreremo la' e poi abbiamo intenzione di andare alla Cattedrale la mattina di Pasqua per la Messa e per il famoso festivale che si chiama 'Lo scoppio del Carro' che e' molto interessante. Il Vescovo dice la Messa.
(On Easter we will be in Florence, we have friends there that we plan to see, and then we intend to go to the Cathedral on the morning of Easter, to attend Mass, and for the famous festival, called 'The explosion of the cart', which is very interesting. The Bishop will celebrate the Mass.)

Marco: Non so niente di questo festival, di che si tratta?
(I don't know anything about this festival, what is it about?)

Caterina: E' troppo complicato per spiegarlo adesso, te lo spieghero' un altra volta.
(It is too complex to explain it now, I will explain it to you another time.)

Marco: Va bene, ma dimmi, almeno, in quali altri posti andrete?
(OK, but tell me, at least, what other places are you going to?)

Caterina: Spero di poter andare a Lucca, Volterra, San Gimignano, paesi vicino a Firenze, circa un ora di distanza con la macchina che affiteremo.
(I hope to be able to go to Lucca, Volterra, San Gimignano, towns near Florence, about an hour by car, which we will rent.)

NOTES

BASIC ITALIAN
Instructions, Cultural Notes and Conversations

Marco: Ma la tua amica e' contenta di vedere questi posti? Non andate nel Sud?
(Is your friend happy to see these places? Aren't you going to the South?)

Caterina: La mia amica mi lascia decidere perche' sono stata in Italia un paio di volte, e si, abbiamo intenzione di andare anche nel Sud.
(My friend lets me decide, because I have been in Italy a couple of times, and yes, we have intention to go to the South also.)

Marco: Che bel itinerario. Ma se andate nel Sud, certamente volete vedere la costa Amalfitana, vero? Tempo fa c'era un articolo, sulla gita ad Amalfi, nel giornale 'Seattle Times'. L'articolo indicava che e' una bellissima gita ma la strada e' piccola, in salita e piena di curve, e' vero? Ci sei mai stata?
(What a nice itinerary! But if you go South, certainly you want to see the Amalfitan coast. Some time ago there was an article in the 'Seattle Times' about the Amalfi drive. The article said that it was a beautiful outing but the street was small, uphill and full of curves, is it true? Have you ever been there?)

Caterina: Certamente andremo ad Amalfi, si, ci sono stata at Amalfi prima ed e' vero che la strada non e' facile, ma quando si arriva ad Amalfi, la vista e' spettacolare e il paesino e' incantevole. Penso che andremo col pullman.
(Certainly we will go to Amalfi; yes, I was there before and it is true that the drive is not easy, but when one arrives at Amalfi, one sees a spectacular view and a charming town. I think we'll take the bus.)

Marco: Un 'altra buona idea. Spero che scriverai degli appunti su tutti questi posti che visiterai, cosi al tuo ritorno mi puoi parlare a lungo del tuo viaggio.
(Another good idea. I hope that you will write notes on all these places that you will visit, so then when you come back, you can talk to me at lenght about your trip.)

Caterina: Si, certo, te lo prometto. Ma, senti, Marco, perche' non ci pensi e vedi se puoi venire con noi, veramente sarebbe divertente.
(Yes, sure, I promise you. But, listen, Mark, why don't you think it over and see if you can come with us, it would really be fun.)

Marco: L'idea e' buona. Bisogna solo vedere se ho ferie e se ho soldi, ma cerchero' comunque, cerchiamo di incontrarci di nuovo prima che partite, cosi potro' conoscere anche la tua amica.
(The idea is good. I need to see if I have any leave available and money, but I will try it, anyway let's try to meet again before you leave, so then I can meet your friend too.)

Caterina: Va bene, certamente, ti telefonero', Ciao
(ok, sure, I will phone you, bye)

NOTES

Marco: Grazie, Ciao
(Thanks, bye)

Vocabulary:

Sacrificare	(to sacrifice)	sacrificio	(sacrifice)
accennare	(to hint)	accenno	(hint)
media	(average)	usanza	(custom)
appunto	(note)	gita	(outing)
gente	(people)	sacco	(sack or bunch)
entrata	(entrance)	laterale	(lateral)

Esercizio 29:

Complete the following sentences by inserting the correct tense of the verb indicated:

1. La settimana scorsa tutti gli studenti in classe _____ bene l'Italiano
   parlare

2. Il mese prossimo un gruppo di ragazzi dell'Universita' _____ in Spagna.
   andare

3. Parlando di Mario, ecco che _____ Mario.
   arrivare

4. Mi piace tanto andare a fare spese e a te ti _____?
   piacere

5. Mentre Maria parlava al telefono, il campanello _____.
   suonare

6. Abbiamo _____ tante volte al Direttore della Banca, senza successo.
   parlare

7. Avevamo _____ il pranzo, quando arrivo' Michele ed aveva fame.
   finire

8. Mi scusi, Signore, Lei _____ Inglese?
   parlare

9. Bisogna _____ insieme al negozio con una macchina.
   andare

NOTES

CAPITOLO VENTISETTE (27)

La concordanza del participio passato

When the past participle of a verb is used with the auxiliary verb 'avere' or 'essere', it follows different rules, which are explained below:

---

past participle combined with the auxiliary

avere:
    1:- is used in the masculine, sing. when the object follows the verb.

    2. it agrees with object pronoun when the object precedes the verb.

essere:
    1. usually agrees with the subject pronoun.

    2. it agrees with obj. pron. when the verb is preceded by pronouns mi, ti, si, ci, vi, si. (reflexive)

Esempi:

Ho mangiato molti biscotti col cappuccino stamattina.

Ho parlato molto in Italiano stasera in classe.

Ho preso tutti i libri dallo scaffale.

Parlando di Maria, mio fratello l'ha presa all'aeroporto oggi.

Quando il bambino e' stato a casa sua, la Nonna lo ha tenuto sempre in braccio.

Maria e' venuta a casa mia ieri sera.

Oggi siamo andati tutti al cinema.

I ragazzi sono venuti a casa della maestra.

NOTES

Ti sei fatto un bel pranzo.

Mario si e' mangiata tutta la pizza.

To simplify the above rule, the past participle, when used with the auxiliary verb 'avere', is often used in the masculine, sing. when the object pronoun follows the verb. This form is most frequently used. With the auxiliary verb 'essere' the past participle agrees with subject pronoun. This form is most frequently used.

Il mare piaceva molto a Caterina ed ogni volta che andava a trovare l'amica, progettavano sempre, tra altre cose, una gita alla spiaggia, specialmente se era d'estate. L'amica ha detto a Caterina, subito dopo che era arrivata, 'ho trovato una bellissima spiaggia, dove l'acqua e' molto chiara e ci sono molti scogli, e' un posto incantevole.' 'Benissimo,' ha detto Caterina, 'mi ha fatto piacere che ti sei interessata a trovarci un bel posto, hai prenotato una stanza a qualche albergo, cosi potremo stare un paio di giorni alla spiaggia?' 'si, ho prenotato una stanza in un albergo piccolo, vicino alla spiaggia, e mi sono comprato un costume da bagno.' veramente? anch'io mi sono comprato un costume da bagno e mi sono comprata anche una bella borsa da spiaggia.' 'brava, sei pronta per questa gita alla spiaggia, sono contenta.' ha detto l'amica a Caterina.

Translation:

Caterina liked the sea very much and every time she went to visit her friend, they would always plan, among other things, an outing to the beach, especially if it was summer. Her friend said to Caterina, right after she had arrived, 'I have found a beautiful beach, where the water is very clear, and there are many rocks, it is a charming place.' 'Nice,' Caterina said, 'I am glad you took care of finding us a nice place, have you reserved a room in some hotel, so we can stay a couple of days at the beach?' 'yes, I have reserved a room in a small hotel, near the beach, and I have bought myself a bathing suit.' 'really, I, also have bought a bathing suit, and I, also, have bought a nice beach bag.' 'good, you are ready for this outing at the beach, I am glad.' said the friend to Caterina.

Vocabulary:

Spiaggia	(beach)	borsa	(bag, purse)	sabbia	(sand)
vicino	(near)	paio	(couple)	costume da bagno	(bathing suit)
prenotare	(to reserve)	bagno	(bath)	scoglio	(big rock)

NOTES

piacere	(pleasing)	le	(to her)	nuotare	(to swim)
tovaglia	(towel)	cabina	(cabin)	profondo	(deep)

Esercizio 30:

Conjugate the present perfect of the verb 'comprare' using the auxiliary verb 'avere' in the present tense (ho comprato). Repeat the conjugation using the auxiliary verb 'avere' in the imperfect tense (avevo comprato.)

Esercizio 31:

Conjugate the present perfect of the verb 'divertire' using the auxiliary verb 'essere' in the present tense and the reflexive pronouns (mi sono divertito.) Repeat the conjugation using the auxiliary verb 'essere' in the imperfect tense and the reflexive pronouns (mi ero divertito.)

NOTES

BASIC ITALIAN
Instructions, Cultural Notes and Conversations

CAPITOLO VENTOTTO (28)

Frasi idiomatiche

As mentioned previously in this book, it is often not recommended to translate a sentence from English into Italian literally. Each language has its own grammatical structure. This fact cannot be more true that when using idioms. Idioms are ways of saying, specific form of speech peculiar to the usage of a particular language.

This chapter will cover a brief summary of the most common idioms used in the Italian language, including a sentence applying its use in context.

acquolina - water

far venire l'acquolina in bocca - to make one's mouth water.

Quando mia sorella cucina, gli odori mi fanno venire l'acquolina in bocca.
(When my sister cooks, the smells make my mouth water.)

altro - other

ben altro - much more

ci mancherebbe altro - God forbid!

Il viaggio dagli Stati Uniti all'Italia incluse tre cambi d'aereo, ci mancherebbe altro se ci si fosse perduta una coincidenza.
(The trip from the States to Italy included three changes of airplane, God forbid if one loses a connection.)

apparenza - appearance

l'apparenza inganna - appearances are deceiving

Giudicando dall'apparenza, non si pensava mai che la signora era una dottoressa.
(Judging from the appearance, one could never guess that the woman was a doctor.)

avanti - forward

mandare avanti la famiglia - to provide for one's family

Giovanni ha due lavori per mandare avanti la sua famiglia.
(Giovanni has two jobs to provide for his family.)

NOTES

bello - beautiful

che fai di bello? - what are you doing? (Referring to pleasant things)

Parlando al telefono con un amico, si puo' dire: Ciao, come stai, che fai di bello oggi?
(Talking on the phone with a friend, one can say: Hi, how are you, what are you doing today?)

non e' bello quel che e' bello, ma quel che piace - beauty is in the eye of the beholder

E' vero che non e' bello quel che e' bello, ma quel che piace, quel ragazzo puo' piacere solo alla sua madre.
(It's true that beauty is in the eye of the beholder, that guy can only be liked by his mother.)

bocca - mouth

in bocca al lupo - good luck!

restare a bocca aperta - to be dumbfounded

Quando ho sentito della sorpresa, sono rimasta a bocca aperta.
(When I heard about the surprise, I was dumbfounded.)

buono - good

alla buona - simply

buono come il pane - good as gold

un buono a niente - a good for nothing

La famiglia viveva alla buona. C'erano anche due fratelli, uno era buono come il pane e l'altro era un buono a niente.
(The family lived simply. There were also two brothers, one was as good as gold and the other a good for nothing.)

cane - dog

cane che abbaia non morde - barking dogs don't bite

da cani - very badly or poorly

fa un freddo cane - the weather is as cold as ice

solo come un cane - completely alone

NOTES

BASIC ITALIAN
Instructions, Cultural Notes and Conversations

In un piccolo paese in montagna c'era un uomo che faceva una vita da cani, abitava in un posto dove faceva un freddo cane e spesso era solo come un cane.

(In a little town in the mountains, there was a man who lived his life very poorly, he lived in a place where the weather was as cold as ice and often he lived completely alone.

carne - meat

ne' carne ne' pesce - neither fish nor fowl

Leggendo l'articolo, non si riconosce il problema. Questo articolo non e' ne' carne ne' pesce, lo scrittore non prende una posizione.
(Reading the article, one does not recognize the problem. This article is neither fish nor fowl, the writer does not take a position in the issue.)

caso - chance

caso mai - if by chance

per caso - by the way

essere il caso - to be appropriate

fare caso - to notice

Se caso mai vai al negozio, comprami il sale. Per caso hai una matita? Non e' il caso di uscire oggi, piove. Hai fatto caso al negozio nuovo?
(If by chance you go to the store, buy me salt. By the way do you have a pencil? It is not appropriate to go out today, it is raining. Have you noticed the new store?)

cuore - heart

al cuore non si comanda - the heart rules or follow your heart

La famiglia non era molto contenta quando la figlia sposo' uno straniero, ma purtroppo al cuore non si comanda.
(The family was unhappy when the daughter married a foreigner, but unfortunanately she followed her heart.)

fare - to make, to do

far si che - to work things out

fare in modo che - to work things out

Luigi ha fatto si che (or in modo che) che e' potuto partire.

NOTES

(Luigi worked things out so he could leave.)

farsi i fatti propri - to mind one's own business

Non ti preoccupare di questo, fatti i fatti tuoi.
(Do not worry about this, mind your own business.)

gatta - cat (fem)

tanto va la gatta al lardo che ci lascia lo zampino - Don't press your luck

gatto - cat (masc.)

quando il gatto non c'e' i topi ballano - When the cat is away the mice will play

Quando il gatto non c'e' i topi ballano, e' proprio vero. Quando i genitori di Cecilia erano fuori citta', lei invito' molti amici a casa sua.
(When the cat is away the mice will play, is really true. When Cecilia's parents were out of town, she invited many friends to her house.)

gente - people

gente allegra, il cielo li aiuta - happy people the sky will help

giorno - day

al giorno d'oggi - nowadays

giro - turn

nel giro di - in a certain amount of time

Nel giro di tre mesi, finiro' questo libro.
(I will finish this book in three months time.)

li' - there

essere sempre li' - to be the same old story

Parliamo e parliamo e siamo sempre li'.
(We talk and talk and we are at the same point.)

li' per li' - on the spur of the moment

Ieri sera li' per li' decidemmo di andare al cinema.
(Last night on the spur of the moment we decided to go to the movies.)

NOTES

male - bad

>**non c'e' male -** not bad

>**non c'e' di che -** don't mention it

mano - hand

>**a portata di mano -** within reach

>**avere le mani bucate -** one who has a hole in his pockets to burn money

>L'uomo vinse la lotteria ma e' come se avesse le mani bucate, spese tutti i soldi.
>(The man won the lottery but it was as if he had a hole in his pockets because he spent all the money.)

>**dare una mano -** to give a hand

>Il marito da spesso una mano alla moglie.
>(The husband often helps his wife.)

>**farsi la mano -** to get used to

>Se parli spesso Italiano, ci fai la mano.
>(If you talk Italian often, you will get used to it.)

>**fuori mano -** out of the way

>**stare con le mani in mano -** to twiddle one's thumbs

mondo - world

>**caschi il mondo -** no matter what

>**cose dell'altro mondo -** unbelievable

>**vivere nel mondo dei sogni -** to have one's head in the clouds

>La studentessa in classe sembrava di vivere nel mondo dei sogni.
>(The student in class appeared to have her head in the clouds.)

occhio - eye

>**l'occhio vuole la sua parte -** appearances count

>Non e' abbastanza essere intelligente, mettiti un bel vestito, l'occhio vuole la sua parte.
>(It is not enough to be intelligent, wear a nice dress, appearances count.)

NOTES

lontano dagli occhi, lontano dal cuore - out of sight, out of mind

Il fidanzato era dovuto partire e lei ha paura che lontano dagli occhi, lontano dal cuore.
(The boyfriend had to leave and she was afraid that out of sight, out of mind!)

pena - punishment

    a mala pena   -   barely

    far pena   -   to feel sorry

    valere la pena-   to be worth the trouble

Per completare questo lavoro ci vuole tanto tempo che non vale la pena farlo.
(To complete this job it takes so much time that it is not worth it.)

serio - serious

    fare sul serio   -   to mean business

    sul serio   -   seriously

Non gioco, faccio sul serio.
(I am not joking, I mean it.)

solo - alone

    meglio soli che male accompagnati -   better alone than in bad company

Ricordati, figlio mio! E' meglio star soli che male accompagnati.
(Remember, my son! It is better to be alone than in bad company.)

    sol soletto -   all by oneself

stanco - tired

    stanco morto -   dead tired

tanto - as or so much

    di tanto in tanto   -   every so often or from time to time

    ogni tanto -   every now and then

tardi - late

    chi tardi arriva male alloggia   -   He, who arrives late, is ill served.

NOTES

uovo - egg

meglio un uovo oggi che una gallina domain - a bird in the hand is worth two in the bush

verso - cry, way

non esserci verso - no way

Puoi parlare a Mario tutto il giorno ma non c'e' verso che lo convinci.
(You can talk to Mario all day but there is no way you can convince him.)

vivo - alive

farsi vivo - to show up

Ti prego, Maria, fatti viva.
(Please Mary come over)

voce - voice

sottovoce - in a low voice

There are many more idioms available, but for the most part, the idioms above are used fairly well in everyday conversations. The student will benefit his knowledge of the language by memorizing a few idioms at a time and incorporating them in sentences, both written and spoken.

Esercizio 32:

Memorize any ten of above idioms and their meaning. Write ten sentences using the memorized idioms.

NOTES

BASIC ITALIAN
Instructions, Cultural Notes and Conversations

CAPITOLO VENTINOVE (29)

Come ordinare un pranzo e come comprare un biglietto per il treno

As mentioned in chapter twelve, the dinner time is a very special time for the average Italian. Time to share daily events with one another. The average meal takes at least one hour to consume on an average, with family. When entertaining friends or relatives, the 'cena' is a preferred time or on Sundays early afternoon, about one thirty or two o'clock. Sundays is often chosen particularly when celebrating an occasion such as a birthday or baptism or any other occasion.

There are different types of restaurants, the good ones cost more, as is every where. 'Tavola calda' (hot table-meaning fast hot foods) restaurants are available, especially in tourist spots. The main thing to remember is that in an italian restaurant one orders food by one course at a time. Usually one begins with a 'primo piatto' a pasta or soup dish, along with a choice of wine, water; bread is often served, without asking for it. At the completion of the first course, the waiter will come back and ask for other orders, if so desired. It is possible to order the whole dinner at the same time if one wishes to do so, but it will still be served one course at a time.

Following is a sample of a brief conversation between a waiter and a tourist in typical italian restaurant:

Come ordinare un pranzo in un ristorante italiano:

Cameriere: Buongiorno, prego, si accomodino.
(Good morning, please, come in.)

Turista: Buongiorno, si, grazie
(Good morning, yes, thank you)

Cameriere: Allora, sono pronti per ordinare? Che cosa desiderano?
(Now then, are you ready to order? What would you like?)

Turista: Che cosa ci raccomanda?
(What do you recommend?)

Cameriere: Tutto e' buono, ma i tortellini alla panna sono veramente buoni.
(Everything is good, but the tortellini with whipping cream are very good.)

Turista: Benissimo, allora prendiamo i tortellini con panna per primo.
(Fine, we will have the tortellini with whipping cream for the first course.)

NOTES

Cameriere:	Va bene, e per secondo? (OK, and for the next course?)
Turista:	Possiamo ordinare dopo per il secondo? (Can we order afterward for the second course?)
Cameriere:	Ma certamente, ritornero' dopo per prendere l'ordinativo. (But, surely, I will come back later to take the order.)
Turista:	Ci porti anche dell'acqua minerale e la lista dei vini, per piacere? (Will you bring us some mineral water and the wine list, please?)
Cameriere:	Certamente. (Certainly)
Cameriere:	Ecco la lista dei vini. (Here is the wine list.)

The bill will include the cover charge per customer, the ordered dishes charged individually, beverages and a ten to fifteen percent service fee. Usually one leaves an additional small tip (mancia) for the waiter. There may be places where a restaurant will advertise an all inclusive dinner for a certain prize, this may vary from place to place and it is more likely to find such an advertisement in tourist spots.

In Italy in addition to the many restaurants, there are many coffee shop, called 'bar'. It is very popular in Italy to stop, on the way to any where, and have an espresso or cappuccino and a pasta (pastry). The espresso is served quickly and is consumed quickly because, usually, the demitasse cup with the espresso coffee is only half full, unless it is ordered 'caffe' macchiato' meaning with a touch of milk, and in that case the cup is two thirds full. Italians normally will order a cappuccino in the morning or late night, because it is filling and they don't want it to interfere with dinner. Dinners hours are at one or so and supper (cena) at eight at night. There is only one kind of cappuccino available and it is delicious. There are bars with stand up room only and some with the option of a table. When the option of the table is chosen, the waiter will come to the table for the order and again there will be a cover charge plus the price of the items. When choosing to stand up, one must pay first at the 'Cassa' (Cashier), receive a receipt and take it to the counter, repeating the items needed to the bartender and consuming them while standing.

The trains in Italy are pretty organized and fast. It is the most common way of traveling throughout Europe. If one studies the system briefly, it will be a big help for traveling by train. The train system is run by the State, therefore the employees at the various stations are always very busy and facing long lines of people. It helps if a consumer is flexible with the dates and times of departure when buying a ticket at the 'biglietteria' (ticket office). Tickets can be purchased in advance and it is recommended to do so. The lines at the stations vary from station to station, the most popular being Rome, Florence, Milan and so forth. Train tickets can be purchased also at a traveling agency, usually a service fee is added.

NOTES

BASIC ITALIAN
Instructions, Cultural Notes and Conversations

Recently there are two most used types of trains, which are called 'Eurostar' and 'Intercity'. The first one is fairly new, clean, nice. It costs a little more that the other, but it is worth it, as the seats are larger, more confortable and the train does not stop in as many places as the other. Also on the 'Eurostar' the price includes the seat, which will be reserved for the ticket holder, and it is mandatory to have reservation for a seat when purchasing a ticket on the 'Eurostar'. With the 'Intercity' type train, it takes longer to arrive at destination because it stops at every little town on the way, the reservation for the seat is optional, so there might be a lot of people sitting on the foldable seats in hallways. The 'Intercity' train has compartments, holding six seats, but it also has one car, usually reserved for people with no seat reservation, usually students traveling home during school breaks.

At all stations there are large signs (cartelloni) for arrivals (arrivi) and departures (partenze), which are updated very frequently. A word of caution, usually the train will be listed with the final destination, while your destination might be different and therefore sooner than the one listed. When purchasing the ticket it is also prudent to make sure the train chosen goes all the way to where you want to go without changing train on the way. Travelers help each other all the time, therefore it is helpful to ask questions if one is not sure. One more important point, at all stations there are small machines, close to the each track, where a traveler must punch the ticket prior to boarding the train, otherwise a fine will be assessed on the train by the ticket checker. This function is relatively new and is called 'obliterare il biglietto' (to obliterate, or punch the ticket).

When all is said and done, traveling by train is a delightful experience, very confortable and very scenic. Beautiful country and city landscapes go by as one travels by train and most often conversations with other travelers occur very frequently, especially among Italians.

Following is a sample of of a brief conversation between a traveler and a ticket employee at a ticket office (biglietteria).

Per comprare un biglietto per il treno da Roma a Firenze:

Viaggiatore: (traveler)   **Per piacere desidero comprare un biglietto per Firenze.**
   (Please I wish to buy a ticket for Florence.)

Impiegato: (clerk)   **Quando desidera andare?**
   (When do you wish to go)

Viaggiatore: **Domani mattina verso le dieci (10 a.m.)**
   (Tomorrow morning around 10 a.m.)

Impiegato: **C'e' un treno alle dieci e diciotto (10:18) ma e' un 'Intercity'**
   (There is one at 10:18 a.m. but it is an 'Intercity')

NOTES

BASIC ITALIAN
Instructions, Cultural Notes and Conversations

Viaggiatore:	No, grazie, desidero un 'Eurostar' e carrozza non fumatori. (No, thanks, I would like an 'Eurostar' and a non smoking car)
Impiegato:	Va bene, c'e' un treno 'Eurostar' alle undici e ventidue (11:22) che va a Firenze. (OK, there is an 'Eurostar' at 11:22 that goes to Florence)
Viaggiatore:	Benissimo, lo prendo, quanto costa? (Fine, I will take it, how much?
Impiegato:	Costa cinquanta (50) mila lire, incluso la prenotazione, come paga? (It costs 50 thousand lire, including the reservation, how will you pay?)
Viaggiatore:	Posso pagare con la carta di credito? (Can I pay with credit card?)
Impiegato:	Si, certo, che tipo 'Visa'? (Yes, sure, what kind, 'Visa')
Viaggiatore:	No, non e' 'Visa', e' 'Mastercard' va bene? (No, it is not 'Visa', it is 'Mastercard' is it OK?)
Impiegato:	Si, certo, ecco la bolletta, prego, la firma. (Yes, sure, here is the receipt, please sign it)
Viaggiatore:	Ecco, grazie. Mi scusi, a che ora arriva a Firenze ed e' diretto? (Here, thanks. Excuse me, at what time does the train arrive in Florence and is it direct?)
Impiegato:	Arriva alle due e quaranta (2:40 p.m.). (It arrives at 2:40 p.m.)
Viaggiatore:	Da che binario parte? (From what track does it leave?)
Impiegato:	Deve guardare sul cartellone delle partenze. (You must look on the departures sign)
Viaggiatore:	Va bene, grazie. (Fine, thanks)

Practice reading aloud both conversations in this chapter.

NOTES

BASIC ITALIAN
Instructions, Cultural Notes and Conversations

CAPITOLO TRENTA (30)

Storielle

Lunedi in Albis

Era quasi tradizionale andare fuori per una scampagnata il Lunedi dopo Pasqua, veniva chiamata 'Lunedi in albis' o Pasquetta.
La giovanetta era molto ansiosa di andare a questa gita ogni anno. Spesso si trattava di una riunione di tutta la famiglia e amici, e, di solito, si andava in un bel posto in campagna oppure in campagna di qualche famigliare, dove si poteva trovare molto spazio all'aperto con erba e alberi. Era un'occasione di felicita'.

Siccome la maggior parte della gente che festeggiava il 'Lunedi in albis' in questo modo, era gente che abitava in appartamenti nei palazzi, ed era stanca di scalini di marmo e mattonelle sui pavimenti. Questa gente era contentissima di avere l'opportunita' di cambiare il programma quotidiamo per un giorno ed andare all'aria aperta per godersi la semplicita' e la bellezza di una campagna o un parco.

La giovanetta era ansiosa di iniziare questa gita ed era occupata ad aiutare sua madre e sua sorella per preparare il mangiare da portare. Lei sapeva che molti cugini che non aveva visto da molto tempo, sarebbero venuti. C'era una cugina in particolare che a lei piaceva molto e che lei sperava che sarebbe venuta. Finalmente era ora di andare. Il posto era una piccola campagna, che apparteneva ad un parente. C'era una tavola lunga che venne subito coperta con un mesale e il cibo venne messo su per tutti i partecipanti. C'era gente dappertutto, c'erano parenti, amici, amici di amici. C'era un pallone e uno spazio per giocare il calcio, e una corda che si usava come altalena ed una rete che si poteva usare per giocare a palla a volo, con un altro pallone. C'erano sentieri per camminare ed alberi erano in abbondanza, alcuni con fiori di primavera e altri con frutta, o, almeno, cominciava a crescere la frutta.

La giovanetta che si chiamava Paolina aveva gia' trovato la cugina, per cui aveva molta simpatia ed aveva gia' cominciato a parlare molto animatamente. Sembravano due vecchie amiche che non si erano viste da molto tempo.

Le due ragazze cominciarono a camminare verso una zona piena di alberi e che sembrava attraente abbastanza da voler esplorarla. Quando arrivarono, trovarono un gruppo di ragazzi che giocavano a calcio. Ci volle solo una sguardo verso Paolina per il giovanotto, che si chiamava Biagio, per decidere che la voleva conoscere. Anche Paolina aveva notato Biagio. I due si scambiarono sguardi, mentre agivano molto timidamente. Era la prima volta che ognuno dei due aveva un'esperienza simile e nessuno dei due sapeva come comportarsi. L'unica cosa che potevano pensare era che ognuno voleva conoscere e stare con l'altro.

NOTES

Biagio perse interesse nella partita di calcio, e stava disperatamente cercando un modo o una scusa per poter parlare con Paolina. Lei, mentre continuava a parlare con la cugina, cercando di agire normalmente, lo guardava furtivamente. Finalmente accadde, si incontrarono, entrambi continuando ad agire molto timidamente.

Biagio e Paolina andarono con un gruppo di giovani ad esplorare i dintorni della campagna. Sebbene essi erano in un gruppo, per ognuno dei due era come se fossero gli unici al mondo.

Era amore a prima vista? Era il primo amore? Durera'?

Solo col passar del tempo si puo' concepire una risposta.

Traduzione:

It was customary to go to a picnic on the Monday after Easter, called 'Lunedi in Albis'. The young woman looked forward to this outing every year. Most of the time, it was a happy family and friends gathering and it would take place somewhere in the country, or at some relative's farm, where there was a lot of open spaces and lots of grass and trees. It was a happy occasion.
Since most of the people, who celebrated Easter Monday this way, were people who lived in apartment buildings, tired of marble steps and tiled floors; they were happy and appreciative to have the opportunity to escape the routine of life for a a day and go to the simplicity and the beauty of a farm or park.

The young woman was anxious to get going to the outing and was busy helping her mother and sister to prepare the food to take. She knew that several cousins whom she had not seen in a long while, would be there. There was one cousin in particular, whom she liked very much and hoped she would be among those who were coming to the outing. Finally it was time to go. The place was a small farm, which belonged to a relative. There was a long table, which was promptly covered with a tablecloth and the food began to be placed on it for all to have. But most of all, there people every where, relatives, friends, and friends who brought friends. There was a ball and an area to play soccer, a rope serving as 'altalena' (swing set) and a net set up for volleyball. Trails for walking were also there and trees were plentiful, some with spring flowers and some with fruit, or, at least, the beginning of fruit.

The young woman, whose name was Paolina, had already found the cousin, whom she liked more than the others, and they started chatting away happily, like two old friends do, especially when they have not seen each other for a while.

NOTES

The two girls began walking among the trees toward an area, which looked nice enough to explore. By the time they reached the area, they found a group of young men playing soccer. It only took one look for the young man, whose name was Biagio, toward Paolina, to know he wanted to meet her. The two exchanged furtive looks toward one another, while behaving in a very shy manner. It was the first time that each of them had felt anything like this and did not know how to deal with it. All each of them knew was that he and she wanted to be with the other.

Biagio soon lost interest in the soccer game he was playing and was searching for a way to meet and talk to Paolina. She, on the other hand, kept talking with her cousin, trying to act normally, but every chance she had, she would look at him. Finally it happened, they met, each acting very shy.

Biagio and Paolina went off with a group of young people, exploring the countryside. Eventhough they were in a group, for each of them, it was as though they were the only two people on earth.

Was it love at first sight? Was it puppy love? Will it last?

Only time could tell.

Le opportunita' della vita

Il cuore della storia avviene in un treno. Una conversazione molto animata tra passeggeri per un tragitto di ore. Queste persone non si erano mai visti prima di salire su questo treno e venire a capitare di sedersi accanto.

Era un 'Intercity' che e' un treno vecchio con corridoi molto stretti e compartimenti dove c'erano sei posti, tre opposti ad altri tre. Questo tipo di treno si fermava ad ogni fermata della rotta destinata. Nei corridoi c'erano sedili piegabili contro il muro per uso per la gente che non ha pagato per un posto riservato.

Nel compartimento, da un lato c'era un uomo di media eta', ben vestito e ovviamente per bene. Vicino a lui c'era una ragazza che era una studentessa di comunicazione, ed era al secondo anno all'Universita' di Perugia. A fianco c'era un giovane, di una trentina d'anni, che sia dal modo di vestire che dal modo di agire, era facile determinare che era un lavoratore. Lui era anche un buon chiaccherone. E' di solito molto facile iniziare una conversazione in questo tipo di situazione, specialmente su un treno, il cui tragitto dura ore.

NOTES

Nei sedili opposti, vicino alla finestra, c'era una ragazza, studentessa di legge, al terzo anno all'Universita' di Roma. Lei era attraente, alta con capelli lunghi e scuri e sembrava molto sicura di se stessa. A fianco a lei, c'era una signora ben vestita e per bene e di eta' avanzata, che parlava poco. Vicino a lei, c'era una giovane con capelli lunghi biondi, belli, molto piccola. Anche lei era una studentessa. Studiava medicina e frequentava l'Universita' di Siena. A volte l'apparenza inganna, ma dal modo di agire e dal modo di parlare una persona dimostra che tipo e'.

Le studentesse cominciarono a parlare tra di loro, sebbene non si conoscevano. Parlarono principalmente riguardo la vita d'Universita' e le caratteristiche della citta' dove era l'Universita' e programmi disponibili ad ogni scuola. Tutte e tre le ragazze tornavano a casa per le feste di Pasqua.

Il giovane lavoratore comincio' a parlare in generale, ma sopratutto si lamentava di varie cose. Era ovvio che la sua vita fin'ora non gli era stata facile. La prima cosa che comincio' a criticare era l'uso della cellullare. Spiego' una situazione in cui una signora vicino a lui parlava al telefonino col tono normale e lui dovette soffire le consequenze, cioe' ascoltare ad una conversazione che non gli interessava, notando, con noia, i vari livelli di voce che occorrono durante una conversazione fra due persone. Inoltre, comincio' a parlare delle sue condizioni di vita, soggetto che colse l'attenzione degli altri passeggeri nel compartimento. Il giovane spiego' che originalmente era di un paese piccolo del Sud e per migliorare ando' a vivere nel Nord per un paio di anni. Trovo' lavoro ma non guadagnava molto. Trovo' una camera che condivideva con un altro lavoratore per risparmiare. Ma cio' nonostante, non ci si trovava e non aveva abbastanza soldi per fare una vita migliore di quella di prima. Ragionava che doveva stare via dalla famiglia e amici, il cibo, le usanze erano diverse dalle sue e la vita nel Nord era piu costosa di quella del Sud. Ad un certo punto si rifiuto' di continuare e abbandonando ogni speranza nel futuro, decise di ritornare al suo paese d'origine e riprendere il modo di vivere di prima sperando di ritrovare il vecchio lavoro o uno simile. Era chiaro che il giovane era deluso e senza molte speranze per un futuro migliore.

Divento' difficile per le altre persone presenti che sentirono tutta la storia, non avere sentimenti di pena verso quest'uomo. Ma sopratutto il contrasto delle condizioni di vita tra questo giovane e le studentesse era enorme ed ovvio. Le opportunita' nella vita, sebbene, esistono per tutti, sono diverse per ogni persona.

Traduzione:

Opportunities in Life

The heart of the story takes place on a train. A very lively conversation between passengers during a train ride lasting several hours. These people had never met before getting on this train e sitting next to each other.

NOTES

It was an 'Intercity', an old type of train with narrow hallways and compartments with six seats, three facing the other three. This type of train would stop at every stop on its route. In the hallways there were foldable seats against the wall to be used by people who had not paid for a reserved seat.

In the compartment on one side there was a middle aged man, well dressed e obviously well to do. Near him there was a girl, who was a communication student and a sophomore at the University of Perugia. Next to her there was a young man, about thirty years old or so, who, by the way he was dressed and by his behaviour, was clearly a laborer. He was also a talker. Usually it is very easy to initiate a conversation in this type of environment, especially on a train ride, whose course lasts hours.

In opposite seats, near the window, there was a girl, law student, a junior at the University of Rome. She was attractive, tall with long and dark hair and appeared very self confident. Next to her there was a lady, well dressed and well to do, perhaps in her sixtys, who spoke very little. Near her there was a young lady with long beautiful, blond hair, she was petite. She was also a student. She was studying medicine and attended the Univeristy of Siena. At times appearances are deceiving, but by the way one talks and behaves one gives away what type of person one is.

The students began talking among themselves, even though they did not know each other. They talked primarily about University life and the characteristics of the city in which their school was located and the programs available. All three of them were going home for Easter holidays.

The young laborer began to talk in general, but mainly he would complain about different things. It was obvious that life had not been easy for him so far. The first thing he began to criticize was the use of cellular phones. He explained a situation in which a woman, near him, was talking on the cellular with a normal voice and he had to suffer the consequences, meaning he had to listen to a conversation that was of no interest to him. He was also annoyed by the various levels of voice that occur during a conversation between two people.

Furthermore, he began to speak about his way of life, a subject that caught the attention of the other passengers in the compartment. The young man explained that he originally was from a small town in the South and to improve his way of life, he went to live in the North for a couple of years. He found work but did not earn very much. He found a room that he shared with another laborer in order to save money. But all to no avail, he was not confortable and did not earn enough to live a better life than the one he had before. He would rationalize that he had to be away from family and friend, the food and customs were different than his own and life in general was more expensive in the North. After thinking it over, he refused to continue this way, abandoning every hope for the future, and decided to return to his original town and live the way he used to, hoping to find work again, either at his old job or something similar. It was clear that the young man was disillusioned and without any hope for a better future.

NOTES

It became difficult for the other people present, who heard the whole story, not to feel sorry for the man. But, mainly, the contrast of the way of life, between this young man and any of the three students there, was huge and obvious. The opportunities in life, eventhough they exist for everyone, they are different for everyone.

Guidare in Italia

Guidare in Italia non e' facile. Anzi e' molto stressante, difficile e disordinato. Ci sono molte macchine, specialmente negli ultimi anni, e le strade sono ancora strette. Naturalmente il peggio e' nelle citta' grandi come Firenze, Roma, Napoli, eccetera. Il pargheggio nei centri popolati e' molto difficile a trovare e a volte bisogna lasciare le chiavi in macchina o con l'attendente. In genere le macchine sono piccole e vecchie, quindi se avviene un urto leggero non e' una tragedia ed e' possibile che il colpevole non si ferma neanche.

Anche sulle autostrade non ci si rimane sempre nella corsia o l'altra, ma spesso ci si guida fra le due. Tutti o la maggior parte degli Italiani guidano cosi, incluso i guidatori di mezzi pubblici. Ci sono molti pullman, che funzionano bene e, di solito, frequentemente trai i posti piu' popolari di ogni citta'.

Esistono in Italia, come altrove in Europa, molte piazze grandi con strade che sbocciano in piazza e che vanno in diverse direzioni. Non e' strano vedere una piazza, per esempio, con una statua al centro, e sei o otto strade che sbocciano in piazza, e bisogna attraversare la piazza per andare sulla strada necessaria. Infatti e' quasi un passatempo sfizioso per un turista stare fermo e osservare questo traffico. E' sbalorditivo.

A vedere il traffico come funziona ed a notare quanti quasi incidenti occorrono, bisogna ammettere che gli Italiani sono buoni guidatori. Dal modo di guida, uno potrebbe concludere che la quota di incidenti per macchine e' alta, invece non lo e' affatto. Incidenti minori ci saranno abbastanza, ma quelli seri non sono molti, rispetto al numero di macchine sulle strade, tenendo conto anche delle condizioni delle strade.

In genere gli Italiani sono molto espressivi e dimostrano le emozioni che sentono. Quando succede che c'e' un incidente non serio, e' possibile che i due guidatori si arrabbiano a vicenda e si bisticciano. Ad osservare una simile situazione, e' facile assumere che la situazione peggiorera' e che i due finiranno all'ospedale. Invece, dopo aver espresso la rabbia in parole l'uno con l'altro, ognuno torna alla propria macchina e continua il suo itinirario, dimenticandosi dell'incidente entro pochi minuti.

NOTES

BASIC ITALIAN
Instructions, Cultural Notes and Conversations

Infine guidare in Italia non e' facile, anzi e' difficile ma e' un'avventura. Un'avventura spesso piacevole, una volta imparato le regole e il modo di guidare delle persone locali. Un turista si puo' godere di belle esperienze guidando da citta' a citta', attraversando bellezze naturali e paesaggi.

Approfittando di guidare fuori mano un turista puo' avere l'opportunita' di conoscere gente locale, tramite qualche ristorante, o alberghetto che si trova in qualche posto fuori mano, ed avere la possibilita' di conversare in Italiano.

Traduzione:

Driving in Italy

Driving in Italy is not easy. On the contrary, it is stressful, difficult and without order. There are many cars, especially in the last few years, and the streets are still narrow. Of course the worst is in the big cities, such as Florence, Rome, Naples, etcetera. The parking in the busiest places is very difficult to find and, at times, it is necessary to leave the keys in the car or with the attendant. For the most part the cars are small and old, so if a minor accident occurs it is not a tragedy and it is even possible that the guilty party will not even stop.

Also on the freeways a driver does not stay within a lane or the other, but, often, between the two. All or the majority of Italian drive this way, including the drivers of public transportation. There are many buses, which function very well and, usually, frequently between popular places in each city.

In Italy, as elsewhere in Europe, there are many large squares with streets opening in the square and going in different directions. It is not unusual to see a square, for example, with a statue in the center, and six or eight streets opening in the circle, and it is necessary to cross the square to go to the necessary street. Infact it is, almost, a fun pastime for a turist to stop at a corner and observe this traffic. It is amazing.

To see how the traffic functions and to note how many near accidents occcur, it is necessary to admit that the Italians are good drivers. From the way they drive one could conclude that the rate of accidents is high, while the opposite is true. There are plenty of minor accidents, but not serious ones relative to the number of cars on the roads, keeping in mind the conditions of the roads.

Generally the Italians are vocal and show their emotions. When a minor accident occurs it is possible that the two drivers get upset with one another and they argue. To observe such a situation, it is easy to assume that the situation will get worse and that the two will end up in some hospital. However, after having expressed their anger in words with one another, they return to their cars and continue their trip, forgetting the whole incident within few minutes.

NOTES

Finally to drive in Italy is not easy, rather it is difficult but it is an adventure. It is an adventure often pleasant, once having learned the rules and the ways of driving of the local people. A tourist could enjoy some beautiful experiences driving from city to city, crossing some beautiful landscapes.

Taking advantage of driving out of the way a tourist could have the opportunity to know local people, through some restaurant or small hotel, possibly located in some out of the way place, and thus have the chance to converse in Italian.

NOTES

BASIC ITALIAN
Instructions, Cultural Notes and Conversations

KEY TO THE EXERCISES

Esercizio 1

1. Finestre
2. Sedie
3. Scrivanie
4. Lavagne
5. Penne
6. Matite
7. Carte
8. Quaderni
9. Libri
10. Tavoli
11. Calcolatori
12. Aggettivi
13. Telefoni
14. Quadri
15. Certificati
16. Ragazzi
17. Scaffali
18. Nipoti
19. Vocali
20. Voci
21. Cucine
22. Pentole
23. Cucchiai
24. Coltelli
25. Piatti
26. Tazze
27. Bicchieri
28. Acque
29. Latte
30. Cappuccini

Esercizio 2

1. La finestra
2. La sedia
3. La scrivania
4. La lavagna
5. La penna
6. La matita
7. La carta
8. Il quaderno
9. Il libro
10. Il tavolo
11. I calcolatori
12. Gli aggetivi
13. I telefoni
14. I quadri
15. I certificati
16. I ragazzi
17. Gli scaffali
18. I nipoti
19. Le vocali
20. Le voci
21. Una cucina
22. Una pentola
23. Un cucchiaio
24. Un coltello
25. Un piatto
26. Una tazza
27. Un bicchiere
28. Un'acqua
29. Un latte
30. Un cappuccino

Esercizio 3

1-e, 2-f, 3-b, 4-c, 5-a, 6-d.

Esercizio 4
1. ha,
2. ha
3. e"
4. ha
5. hanno
6. e'
7. E'
8. e'

Esercizio 5
1-e
2-d
3-b
4-c
5.-a

9. abbiamo
10. Avete

Esercizio 6

1.	Gentili	11.	Queste
2.	Indipendenti	12.	Quelle
3.	Notevoli	13.	Belle
4.	Piacevoli	14.	Buone
5.	Amichevoli	15.	Cattive
6.	Belli	16.	Brutte
7.	Buoni	17.	Dolci
8.	Cattivi	18.	Freschi
9.	Brutti	19.	Freddi
10.	Ultimi	20.	Azzurre

Esercizio 7

1. Buon giorno, 2. Questa sera, 3. Bella mattina, 4. Bel pomeriggio, 5. Brutta notte, 6. Piacevole domani, 7. Buona settimana, 8. Bella stagione, 9. Fredda primavera, 10. Bell'estate.

Esercizio 8

La tovaglia, il tovagliolino, i piatti, le tazze, il cucchiaio, la forchetta, il coltello, la brocca, la forchettina, la tazzina.

Esercizio 9

Stare	Essere	Avere
sto	sono	ho
stai	sei	hai
sta	e'	ha
stiamo	siamo	abbiamo
state	siete	avete
stanno	sono	hanno

Esercizio 10

1. dei
2. col
3. del
4. dello
5. della
6. degli
7. al
8. nel
9. sulla
10. Dalla

BASIC ITALIAN
Instructions, Cultural Notes and Conversations

Esercizio 11

1. La mia penna e' sulla scrivania.
2. Il padre di Maria e' piu' alto del padre di Mario.
3. La mia casa e' bella.
4. La tua casa e' grande.
5. Il suo ufficio ha una finestra.
6. Mio fratello parla Italiano.
7. I miei libri sono sulla scrivania.
8. La loro macchina e' piccola.
9. I prezzi sono altissimi o carissimi.
10. Questo vino e' migliore di quel vino.

Esercizio 12

1. Piu' grande
2. Il piu' piccolo
3. Bellissima, bravissima
4. Vostro, grande
5. Piu' basso
6. Piu' blu
7. Piu' cari
8. Piccolo
9. Alti
10. Cattivi

Esercizio 13

1. Mia sorella abita al primo piano.
2. Mio fratello arriva alle otto di sera.
3. Il vino costa quattro mila lire.
4. Maria ha dieci mele.
5. Quanto costa questo piatto?
6. Il bambino ha tre matite.
7. A che ora comincia il film?
8. Il film comincia alle sette.
9. Questa e' la decima lezione.
10. L'albero e' costoso.

Esercizio 14

Uno
Due
Tre
Quattro
Cinque
Sei
Sette
Otto
Nove
Dieci
Undici
Dodici
Tredici
Quattordici
Quindici

Esercizio 15

1. Parlera', 2. Parlera', 3. Parleranno, 4. Parlerai, 5. Parleremo.

Esercizio 16

1. Tu sarai sul treno, compartimento D, sedile No. 10 per Firenze.
2. Noi avremo una lettera da Maria.
3. Maria avra' un pacco dall'Italia.
4. Giovanni parlava continuamente.
5. Maria parlo' bene in classe.

6. Noi saremo a Roma in Aprile.
7. Maria parlo' bene del viaggio.
8. Mentre Giovanni parlava, il telefono suono'.
9. I ragazzi saranno a casa mia domani.
10. Gli studenti parlarono Italiano in classe.

Esercizio 17

Mi alzo, mi faccio, mi vesto, ti vengo, si divertono, mi dispiace, ci divertiamo.

Esercizio 18

1-a, 2-c, 3-b, 4-f, 5-h, 6-d, 7-k, 8-e, 9-i, 10-g.

Esercizio 19

1. Come stai, 2. Non mi sento bene, 3. Hai, 4. Parliamo, 5. Ci troviamo, 6. Mi piace, 7. Sembrano, si divertono, 8. Si va, 9. Si chiama, 10. Ci siamo divertiti.

Esercizio 20

1-c, 2-e, 3-a, 4-f, 5-l, 6-h, 7-g, 8-i, 9-d, 10-b.

Esercizio 21

Loro, lo, loro, loro, la, compra**la**.

Esercizio 22

1. He eats at the restaurant with her every day.
2. If you don't buy the scarf, I will buy it.
3. I explained that I will phone him at noon.
4. Mario has many friends, he invites them at home.
5. The lady has a dog, do you see it?
6. We give him a hand.

Esercizio 23

1. Compleanno, 2. Ha fatto, 3. Il pranzo, 4. Pasta asciutta, 5. Ha preparato, 6. Italiano, 7. Riunisce, 8. Parla.

BASIC ITALIAN
Instructions, Cultural Notes and Conversations

Esercizio 24

1-e, 2-h, 3-a, 4-b, 5-j, 6-c, 7-d, 8-g, 9-f, 10-i.

Esercizio 25

1. Ha parlato, 2. E' arrivato, 3. Essendo stato, 4. E' rimasto, 5. Sarebbe rimasta, 6. Aveva mangiato, 7. Avendo bevuto, 8. Avesse avuto, 9. Aveva capito, 10. Aveva dimenticato.

Esercizio 26

1. Ricevuto, 2. Fatto, 3. Capito, 4. Scritto, 5. Comprato, 6. Letto, 7. Risposto, 8. Incontrato, 9. Preso, 10. Finito.

Esercizio 27

1. Ti, 2. Mi, 3. Si, 4. Si, 5. Si, 6. Mi, 7. Si, 8. Si, 9. Si, 10. Si, 11. Ci, 12. Si.

Esercizio 28

1. When I arrive in Florence next year, first thing, I would like to go see the Cathedral in town.

2. In order to do an organized trip it is necessary to have an itinerary and follow it.

3. When a person goes to Italy for turism, it is more fun to speak the Italian language and communicate in their language.

4. I would have talked slower, if I knew you did not understand the language.

5. Having talked Italian often with his friends, Mark talked Italian very well during his trip to Italy last month.

6. The professor was talking about history in detail.

7. When you call me on the phone, I do not understand the language very well.

8. I hope I will be able to talk Italian well enough to be able to understand the Italian, when I go to Italy next year.

9. In Florence there are many museums to visit, also the Cathedral, the Baptistery and Giotto tower and many other things.

10. There are many nice stores in Naples, where the people can shop and talk with the salespeople

Esercizio 29

1. Parlarono, 2. Andranno, 3. Arriva, 4. Piace, 5. Suono', 6. Parlato, 7. Finito, 8. Parla, 9. Andare.

Esercizio 30

Ho comprato, hai comprato, ha comprato, abbiamo comprato, avete comprato, hanno comprato, avevo comprato, avevi comprato, aveva comprato, avevamo comprato, avevate comprato, avevano comprato.

Esercizio 31

Mi sono divertito, ti sei divertito, si e' divertito, ci siamo divertiti, vi siete divertiti, si sono divertiti. Mi ero divertito, ti eri divertito, si era divertito, ci eravamo divertiti, vi eravate divertiti, si erano divertiti.

ABOUT THE AUTHOR

Imma Trisorio Keith was born and raised in Naples, Italy. She migrated to the United States where she received a Bachelor of Science degree in Business Administration from the University of Southern Mississippi. She started teaching Italian to Navy personnel deploying to Italy. She has been teaching for the past 15 years. Currently she teaches classes and tutors individuals in Italian language.